Oxford

AMERICAN DICTIONARY
VOCABULARY BUILDER

Keith Folse

OXFORD

UNIVERSITY PRESS

OXFORD
UNIVERSITY PRESS

Great Clarendon Street, Oxford OX2 6DP

Oxford University Press is a department of the University of Oxford.
It furthers the University's objective of excellence in research, scholarship,
and education by publishing worldwide in

Oxford New York

Auckland Cape Town Dar es Salaam Hong Kong Karachi
Kuala Lumpur Madrid Melbourne Mexico City Nairobi
New Delhi Shanghai Taipei Toronto

With offices in

Argentina Austria Brazil Chile Czech Republic France Greece
Guatemala Hungary Italy Japan Poland Portugal Singapore
South Korea Switzerland Thailand Turkey Ukraine Vietnam

OXFORD and OXFORD ENGLISH are registered trade marks of
Oxford University Press in the UK and in certain other countries

© Oxford University Press 2011

The moral rights of the author have been asserted

Database right Oxford University Press (maker)

First published 2011

2015 2014 2013 2012 2011

10 9 8 7 6 5 4 3 2

ISBN: 978 0 19 439995 1

Printed in China

ACKNOWLEDGMENTS

*The publisher would like to thank the following for their kind permission to
reproduce photographs and other copyright material:* Oxford University Press
pp1 (puppy/Ingram), 3 (racket/Photodisc), 5 (autumn/Digital Vision), 6
(ice skates, rollerblades, rollerskates, skateboard, tractor-trailer/ Hemera
Technologies Inc.), 7 (saucepan/Dorling Kindersley RF), 8 (woman in office/
Blend Images), 9 (party/Blend Images), 10 (shop/image100), 11 (snake/
Photodisc), 12 (parking/Photodisc), 13 (bookshop/Blend Images), 14 (x-ray/
Photodisc), 15 (UFO/Photodisc), 15 (Doctor/Digital Vision), 15 (Mount Fuji/
Photodisc), 15 (internet/1Apix), 16 (woman in coat/Photodisc), 17 (Winter
Palace/Photodisc), 18 (world/Graphi-Ogre), 20 (restaurant/Good Shoot), 21
(alarm clock/Photodisc), 23 (shuttle launch/Photodisc), 24 (dog/Photodisc),
25 (shadows/Photodisc), 26 (trolley/Photodisc), 27 (bear/Photodisc), 28
(gardening/Photodisc), 28 (watching TV/Comstock), 29 (human skeleton/
OUP), 31 (airplane/Photodisc), 32 (gym/Fuse), 33 (parrot/Corel), 36 (barber/
Photodisc), 37 (angle diagrams/Q2A Media), 37 (teacher/Digital Vision), 38
(butterfly/Ingram), 38 (pollen/Photodisc), 38 (fingerprint/Photodisc), 38 (fish/
Corel), 38 (fern/Corbis/Digital Stock), 39 (US flag/Image Farm), 41 (diving
board/Photodisc), 41 (school bus driver/Stockbyte), 41 (oven cleaner/White),
41 (man/Image Source), 43 (sports coach/BananaStock), 43 (laundry/Polka Dot
Images), 44 (woman/Image Source), 46 (ill man/Stockbyte), 47 (sushi/Amana
Images Inc.), 48 (dinner/Blend Images), 49 (book/D. Hurst)

Contents

Preface

Vocabulary is perhaps the single most important component in learning a foreign language. Research has shown a very strong correlation between vocabulary and reading, writing, speaking, and listening, and our learners certainly know that insufficient vocabulary can completely stop their English communication. Despite the obvious importance of vocabulary in mastering a new language, many ESL and EFL programs still lack a systematic and effective approach to vocabulary teaching or learning, in part because of the relative paucity of books offering explicit vocabulary practice for English language learners (ELLs).

The *Oxford American Dictionary Vocabulary Builder* has been designed as a useful learning tool to increase learners' vocabulary as they interact with selected lexical information from the new *Oxford American Dictionary for Learners of English*. To this end, the *OAD Vocabulary Builder* consists of 50 single-page lessons that practice key vocabulary in the following areas: useful dictionary skills, which word (words with similar spellings or meanings), spelling, pronunciation, parts of speech, informal language (including idioms), collocations, content areas (i.e., math, science, social studies, sports), the Oxford 3000™ (a special list of 3,000 essential vocabulary words), and the Academic Word List (570 essential academic vocabulary words).

The *OAD Vocabulary Builder* accompanies the new *Oxford American Dictionary*. All examples in the *OAD* are based on actual language usage from a corpus of more than 2 billion words, so the *OAD* is much more than a mere source of spelling and meanings. This new dictionary is in fact so rich with information about usage, including example sentences, collocations, word grammar, and potential ELL errors, that the *OAD* is more than a traditional dictionary: it is in fact the perfect vocabulary book for ELLs.

As a person who has learned and taught several languages, I know that serious students will welcome the opportunity to interact with the tremendous amount of useful vocabulary in this book. Teachers will appreciate the flexibility of the book's organization in that the 50 lessons can be done in any order. The inclusion of an answer key within the book allows learners to check their own answers, thus permitting independent learning and allowing time in class for learners to work on communicative and/or language recycling activities.

Acquiring a large vocabulary that will enable our learners to comprehend the language around them is an extremely daunting task. Because there is so much vocabulary to be learned, it is impossible for any one book or course to provide all the language that is needed; therefore, the responsibility of this important task must fall on our learners. One encounter with a word is rarely enough to learn the word, but it is often sufficient to raise learners' consciousness of the word so that they are more likely to pay attention to the word when they encounter it in listening or reading. To this end, the *Oxford American Dictionary Vocabulary Builder* helps learners acquire a solid base of vocabulary while helping train them to be active vocabulary seekers.

Keith Folse, Ph.D.
Professor, TESOL
University of Central Florida
January 2011

Locating words in your dictionary Dictionary skills

Your **Oxford American Dictionary** lists all the words in alphabetical order by the first, or initial, letter of the word. When all the words begin with the same initial letter, the first letter that is different determines the order of the words.

> **beach** /bitʃ/ *noun* [C] (**GEOGRAPHY**) the piece of land covered with sand or rocks next to the ocean: *a nice sandy beach • to lie on the beach*
>
> **bea·con** /ˈbikən/ *noun* [C] a fire or light on a hill, a tower, or near the coast, which is used as a signal
>
> **bead** /bid/ *noun* [C] **1** a small ball of wood, glass, or plastic with a hole in the middle for threading a string through **2** a drop of liquid: *There were beads of sweat on his forehead.*
>
> **bea·gle** /ˈbigl/ *noun* [C] a small dog with short legs, sometimes used for hunting
>
> **beak** /bik/ *noun* [C] the hard, pointed part of a bird's mouth ⊃ See picture at **animal**.
>
> **beak·er** /ˈbikər/ *noun* [C] (**CHEMISTRY**) a glass container with a flat bottom, used by scientists for pouring liquids
>
> **beam¹** /bim/ *noun* [C] **1** a line of light: *the beam of a car's headlights • a laser beam* **2** a long piece of wood, metal, etc. that is used to support weight, for example in the floor or ceiling of a building
>
> **beam²** /bim/ *verb* **1** [I] to smile happily: *Beaming with pleasure, she stepped forward to receive her prize.* **2** [I] to send out light and warmth: *The sun beamed down on them.* **3** [T] to broadcast a signal: *The program was beamed live by satellite to many different countries.*

A. Alphabetical order using initial letters

Number these words from 1 to 12 to indicate the order in which they are listed in your dictionary.

.... youth .... onion .... arrow .... reward

.... embarrass .... wrapping .... neat .... joy

.... zero .... fuel .... deaf .... bury

B. Alphabetical order with words starting with the same first letter

Number these words from 1 to 12 to indicate the order in which they are listed in your dictionary.

1. .... flat
.... feather
.... fact
.... flour
.... flow
.... faucet
.... factor
.... fork
.... fasten
.... factory
.... floor
.... form

2. .... owe
.... organized
.... ought to
.... old-fashioned
.... organize
.... old
.... o'clock
.... OK
.... once
.... onion
.... Oct.
.... online

What are **guide words**? In the dictionary you can see at the top of each double-page spread the first and last word on those two pages. These guide words help you locate the words more quickly.

C. Using guide words

Locate each of these words in your dictionary and copy the guide words from the double-page spread where you found the word.

1. **guilty** .... ←→ ....
2. **phase** .... ←→ ....
3. **achieve** .... ←→ ....
4. **raw** .... ←→ ....

5. **seek** .... ←→ ....
6. **remote** .... ←→ ....
7. **dot** .... ←→ ....
8. **upset** .... ←→ ....

D. Timed word search

Work in small groups. Take turns saying one word from the dictionary. See who can find the word and then tell the guide words associated with that word the most quickly.

E. New words

All of the words in this lesson are from the **Oxford 3000** list of keywords. Write down any new words and then look up their definitions.

Word 1. .... = ...

Word 2. .... = ...

Word 3. .... = ...

Understanding an entry Dictionary skills

To find out more about the information in the **Oxford American Dictionary**,
look at the Guide to the Dictionary on pp. vii–ix.

A. Look at these two entries from your **Oxford American Dictionary**.

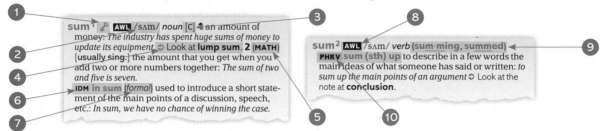

Now match the numbered parts of the dictionary text with **ten** of the fourteen different types
of information listed below.

1 c.   2 ....   3 ....   4 ....   5 ....   6 ....   7 ....   8 ....   9 ....   10 ....

a. Numbers on words with the same spelling but
    different parts of speech

b. Part of speech – noun, verb, etc.

c. An important word belonging to the Oxford 3000

d. An item from the Academic Word List of vocabulary
    used a lot in textbooks and lectures

e. Pronunciation

f. A particular subject area where the word or
    meaning is used

g. Grammar information – countable and uncountable
    nouns, etc.

h. Different meanings of a word

i. A link to a related term

j. Example sentence showing how the word
    is used

k. Help with using the word in particular
    situations – informal, formal, etc.

l. An idiom using the word

m. Forms of a word – parts of the verb, plurals
    of nouns, etc.

n. A phrasal verb using the word

B. Doctor Dictionary

See if you can help solve these problems. In each case, look up the word in **bold** print
and give the answer to the problem. Then say which feature of the dictionary entry
gave you the answer. You have to choose one of the features listed below.

| a. syllable dots | b. derivatives | c. stress marks | d. preposition used after a word |
| e. opposites | f. other ways of saying something | g. irregular plurals | |

	What's the problem?	What's the answer?	Where's the answer?
1.	Do you say <u>veg</u>etable or veg<u>e</u>table?		
2.	Is there an adjective formed from **sugar**? I want to say "a .... drink".		
3.	Is there a less formal way of talking about a **dormitory**?		
4.	What's wrong with "**Listen** what she says"?		
5.	My sister said something that was not very **kind** – so was it non-kind, inkind, unkind or something else?		
6.	"Baked **potato**" is correct, so I guess "mashed pota<u>tos</u>" is OK, isn't it?		
7.	How do I divide the word "**tomorrow**" into syllables?		

Grammar information Dictionary skills

Most people think of a dictionary as a source of meanings and spelling, but your **Oxford American Dictionary** also has information about the grammar of words.

Countable/Uncountable Nouns
Most noun entries are marked with [C] or [U]. A countable noun has both a singular form and a plural form, and in the singular, it must have an article or determiner in front of it. An uncountable noun has no plural.

Singular/Plural Nouns
Some nouns are marked with [sing.] or [pl.] to show that they are always followed by a singular verb (e.g. **bloodstream**) or a plural verb (e.g. **police**).

Transitive/Intransitive Verbs
Verb entries are marked with [T] or [I] to indicate whether they are transitive and have a direct object, or intransitive, without a direct object.

Other grammar information includes usage (e.g. **deafen** is usually passive and **deserve** is not used in the continuous tenses) and placement (e.g. **awake** is not used before a noun).

> **ad·vice** /əd'vaɪs/ *noun* [U] an opinion that you give someone about what he/she should do: *She took her doctor's advice and quit smoking. ◆ Let me give you some advice … ◆ You should get some legal advice* (= ask a lawyer to tell you what to do).
>
> **GRAMMAR**
>
> Advice is an uncountable noun, so we cannot say "an advice" or "some advices." We can say *a piece of advice* and *a lot of advice*.

A. Use your dictionary to check whether the noun in **bold** is countable or uncountable. Put *a* or *an* in front of it if it is countable, and nothing if it is uncountable.

1. By providing .... **shade**, this tree provides .... **protection** for the delicate flowers at its base.

2. Sue is .... ardent **supporter** of .... new **law** that would ban smoking in all public places.

3. The police arrested the man for .... **arson**, but he said this is .... **crime** he didn't commit.

4. Daniel's father made .... **fortune** in the sale of .... Egyptian **cotton**.

5. It's virtually impossible to repair .... plastic **cup** if it has .... small **leak**.

6. In that area of Europe, ... **castle** is almost always surrounded by .... **moat**.

B. If the verb in **bold** is intransitive, choose the correct preposition that should follow. If the verb is transitive, circle --- to indicate that no preposition can follow it.

1. In the movie, the main character **murders** (at, in, on, ---) her uncle.

2. The team from Lincoln High **walloped** (by, in, with, ---) our school in the game.

3. When I **leaned** (by, for, on, ---) the freshly painted wall, my shirt got paint on it.

4. Everyone considered him to be rude because he didn't **greet** (at, for, to, ---) anyone in the morning.

5. The students **listened** attentively (at, for, to, ---) everything the teacher said.

C. What is wrong with these sentences? Study the entry for the **bold** words, identify the problem and correct the sentences.

1. Kevin loves tennis. He is **avid**. ....

2. Mr. Kilgore gives us three or more **homeworks** every night. ....

3. Your research paper received an F because it is **devoid** in original writing. ....

4. My mom always **says** me to clean up my room. ....

5. The police **hounded** to the suspect until he confessed to the crime. ....

6. That plan will definitely work. It's **sure-fire**. ....

7. Jim has been **paralegal** in a law firm near my office since 1999. ....

8. Do you think these jeans are **suiting** me? ....

9. An amoeba is a very small **alive** creature. ....

10. This **bacteria** causes disease in very hot climates. ....

A dictionary gives the meaning of thousands of words, but your **Oxford American Dictionary** also contains information on words that are similar in meaning to each other.

When there is only one, or sometimes two, words that have a similar meaning, your dictionary lists that word as a synonym with the symbol **SYN** at the end of the definition. In this case, you should check the entry of the synonym to compare meanings and usages.

Your dictionary also lists words with the opposite meaning (antonyms) with the symbol **ANT**.

> **slap**[1] /slæp/ *verb* [T] (**slap·ping, slapped**) **1** to hit someone or something with the inside of your hand: *She slapped him across the face.* ◆ *to slap someone on the back* (= to congratulate him/her) **SYN smack**

> **smack**[1] /smæk/ *verb* [T] to hit someone or something with the inside flat part of your hand: *She smacked him right on the head.* **SYN slap**

> **slow-ˈwitted** *adj.* not able to think quickly; slow to learn or understand things **ANT quick-witted**

A.

1. Give the synonym of each of the following words.

1. **burst** (*verb*) ....
2. **buy sb off** ....
3. **cancel** ....
4. **candid** ....
5. **caress** ....

6. **chief** (*adj.*) ....
7. **drowsy** ....
8. **emphasize** ....
9. **extraordinary** ....
10. **repair** (*verb*) ....

2. Give the antonym of each of the following words.

1. **civilized** ....
2. **cloudy** ....
3. **exhale** ....
4. **final** ....

5. **hospitable** ....
6. **precise** ....
7. **sane** ....
8. **satisfaction** ....

Your dictionary also has Thesaurus boxes, which list groups of words that have a similar meaning. These boxes contain sample sentences and word combinations that help differentiate the usage of these words.

> **THESAURUS**
>
> **look**
>
> glance ◆ gaze ◆ stare ◆ glimpse ◆ glare
>
> These are all words for an act of looking, when you turn your eyes in a particular direction.
>
> **look** an act of looking at someone or something: *Here, take a look at this.* ◆ *Do you want to have a look around?*
>
> **glance** a quick look: *She stole a glance at her watch.*
>
> **gaze** a long steady look at someone or something: *He felt embarrassed under her steady gaze.*
>
> **stare** a long look at someone or something, especially in a way that is unfriendly or that shows surprise: *She gave the officer a blank stare and shrugged her shoulders.*
>
> **glimpse** a look at someone or something for a very short time, when you do not see the person or thing completely: *He caught a glimpse of her in the crowd.*
>
> **glare** a long angry look at someone or something: *She gave her questioner a hostile glare.*
>
> **PATTERNS**
> ■ a look/glance **at** sb/sth
> ■ a **penetrating/piercing** look/glance/gaze/ stare
> ■ a **long** look/glance/stare
> ■ a **brief** look/glance/glimpse

B. Answer the following questions. For help, study the Thesaurus box for the word shown at the end of each sentence.

1. Which is usually the largest – a **property**, a **complex**, or a **structure**? .... **building**

2. Which sounds nicer – **cheap** or **inexpensive**? .... **cheap**

3. When talking to a friend, would you probably say, "I want to **pick** my own present", or "I want to **select** my own present"? .... **choose**

4. If a restaurant serves **lukewarm** coffee, will customers appreciate it? .... **cold**

5. To make a complaint about a dirty hotel room, would you say it was **dusty**, **filthy**, or **grubby**? .... **dirty**

6. **Illness**, **condition**, **bug** – which one is the least serious? .... **disease**

7. Which word is good to describe a freshly baked cake – **moist**, **damp**, **drenched**? .... **wet**

8. What is the best classification of the scientific word "gravity" – a **phrase**, an **idiom**, or a **term**? .... **word**

Selecting the right meaning Dictionary skills

When you look up a word and find more than one meaning listed, it is important to select the meaning that matches the context where you saw or heard the word. For example, you probably know the word **table** as a piece of furniture, but consider this sentence: *The table on page 97 contains the most recent population data*. What does **table** mean here? Is this the first or second meaning in your dictionary?

> **ta·ble¹** ✏ /ˈteɪbl/ *noun* [C] **1** a piece of furniture with a flat top on one or more legs: *a kitchen table* ♦ *a coffee table* ♦ *Could you set the table for lunch?* (= put the knives/forks/plates on it) ♦ *Don't read the newspaper at the table* (= during the meal). ♦ *table manners* (= the way that you behave when you are eating) **2** a list of facts or figures, usually arranged in rows down a page: *a table of contents* ♦ *Table 3 shows the results.*

You can get help in finding the right meaning from the <u>short cuts</u> (see the entry for the noun **game**), the <u>subject labels</u> (see the entry for the noun **bypass**), and the <u>example sentences</u>.

A. The noun **fall** has 5 meanings in your dictionary. Write the number (1, 2, 3, 4, 5) to indicate which meaning of the noun **fall** is used in these sentences.

.... a. In the **fall** of 2008, Jim and I took a trip to Vermont to see the leaves change color.

.... b. The **fall** of the Byzantine Empire occurred in the year 1453.

.... c. Because of his **fall** last week, my grandfather had to go to the hospital.

.... d. Any sudden **fall** in the price of gold can hurt the country's currency.

.... e. Thousands of tourists come to see the spectacular **fall** foliage.

.... f. Some historians say the end of the Berlin Wall began the **fall** of the Soviet Union.

.... g. It's a 30-minute walk to the **falls** from the lodge.

.... h. I can't wait to see the **fall** TV schedule.

.... i. Many homeowners are worried about the **fall** in the value of their property.

B. Use the Word Bank of various meanings of five words (*fan, lighten, messy, mint, pound*) to complete these sentences. The numbers in parentheses refer to the meaning number in your **Oxford American Dictionary**.

> **WORD BANK**
>
> fan¹ (1)   fan¹ (2)   pound¹ (1)   pound¹ (2)   lighten (1)   lighten (2)
> messy (1)   messy (2)   messy (3)   mint (1)   mint (2)   mint (3)

1. I am a huge .... of the New York Yankees.
2. I wish my office weren't so ....
3. The company's profits suffered because of last year's .... strike.
4. You can .... your suitcase by taking out those big boots.
5. The main .... for U.S. money is in Washington, D.C.
6. A British .... is worth more than a dollar.
7. Ask the clerk for a .... of ground beef.
8. Making a pie from scratch can be a very .... task.
9. As dawn approached, the sky began to .... in the east.
10. If you put a .... leaf in iced tea, it tastes great.
11. After dinner at a restaurant, I like to eat a .... to freshen my breath.
12. My bedroom has a ceiling ...., so it's not hot at all in the evenings.

Information from illustrations Dictionary skills

As well as definitions composed of words, your dictionary contains many color illustrations that can help you understand the meaning of a new word. Definitions are helpful, but sometimes a picture is even more valuable.

tractor-'trailer *noun* [C] a very large truck that consists of two connected parts, which can carry a large quantity of things over a long distance **SYN semi** ⊃ See picture at **truck¹**.

tractor-trailer (*also* semi)

A. See the illustrations in your dictionary for the word(s) on the left. Then answer the questions about the illustrations.

1. **bread**
   a. What is the brown outer covering of bread called?
   b. What word means the whole bread before you cut it into slices?

2. **brushes**
   a. Which **three** brushes do you use for brushing or cleaning parts of your body?

   b. When you sweep the floor, what do you brush the dirt into?

3. **chairs**
   a. Which **two** chairs are made for more than one person to sit on?
   b. What type of chair doesn't have arms or a back?

4. **fruit and vegetables**
   a. What do you call the yellow outer covering of a banana?
   b. What are the two main colors of a watermelon?

5. **graphs and charts**
   a. Which of these is round – a bar graph, a flow chart, or a pie chart?
   b. What do we call the two straight lines on a graph?

6. **hats**
   a. What does a construction worker wear – a beret, a hard hat, a top hat?
   b. Name **three** types of hats that have a brim.

7. **kitchen utensils**
   a. Which of these is used to put soup into a bowl – a colander, a ladle, a whisk?

   b. Which do you use when frying a hamburger – a funnel, a peeler, a spatula?

8. **plugs**
   a. Do you insert an outlet into a plug or vice versa?
   b. What comes out of a faucet – air, money, water?

9. **tools**
   a. Which of these is for putting leaves in one place – a drill, a plunger, or a rake?

   b. Which of these is for cutting wood – a hammer, a saw, a screwdriver?

10. **track and field**
    a. When people sprint, do they jump, throw, or run?
    b. Which **two** sports in the picture involve throwing something?

ice skates   in-line skates   roller skates   skateboard

B. Skim your dictionary to find other illustrations. Write **three** new useful words and their meanings here.

Word 1. _____ = _____

Word 2. _____ = _____

Word 3. _____ = _____

Words that look alike #1 Which word

Sometimes two words that look similar are related. Consider the words **hand** and **handle**. They are two different things but these two words are related because a **handle** on a door, drawer, etc. is where you place your **hand** to open it.

However, two words that look similar may be completely unrelated. Consider the words **rival** and **river**. These two words are not at all related.

hand¹ 🔊 /hænd/ *noun*
> PART OF BODY **1** [C] the part of your body at the end of your arm, including your fingers and thumb: *Raise your hand if you know the answer.* ◆ *He took his daughter by the hand.* ◆ *He held the bird gently in the palm of his hand.*

han·dle² 🔊 /ˈhændl/ *noun* [C] a part of something that is used for holding or opening it: *the door handle* ◆ *the handle of a frying pan* ⇨ See picture at **pan¹**.

ri·val¹ 🔊 /ˈraɪvl/ *noun* [C] a person, group, or thing that is competing with another: *They're business rivals.* ◆ *The top candidate has a 3% lead over her closest rival.*

riv·er 🔊 /ˈrɪvər/ *noun* [C] **(GEOGRAPHY)** a large, natural stream of water that goes across the land and into the sea: *the Mississippi River* ◆ *a picnic on the bank of the river*

A. For each pair of similar-looking words taken from the **Oxford 3000**, circle *yes* or *no* to indicate whether you think the meanings of the two words are related or not. Be prepared to explain your answers.

1.	hand – handle	(yes) no	11.	sure – ensure	yes no
2.	rival – river	yes no	12.	injure – injury	yes no
3.	anger – angry	yes no	13.	proper – property	yes no
4.	wide – width	yes no	14.	heal – healthy	yes no
5.	thorough – through	yes no	15.	flow – flower	yes no
6.	visible – vision	yes no	16.	edition – editor	yes no
7.	battle – battery	yes no	17.	power – powder	yes no
8.	online – outline	yes no	18.	statue – status	yes no
9.	shade – shadow	yes no	19.	threat – threaten	yes no
10.	sour – source	yes no	20.	plain – planet	yes no

B. Answer the questions in the space provided. If you need help, look up the **bold** words in your dictionary.

1. On a hot day, do people go to sit in the **shade** or **shadow**? ....

2. Which of these fruit is the most **sour** – grapes, lemons, or grapefruit? ....

3. When writing a report, what is most students' primary **source** of information? ....

4. If you do a **thorough** job with your report, what does that mean? ....

5. If you travel **through** a city, do you take the beltway? ....

6. Which direction does the Mississippi **flow**? North to south or south to north? ....

7. What is the state **flower** of Texas – apple blossom or blue bonnet? ....

8. Are you more likely to shop **online** or to travel **online**? ....

9. Does the **outline** of a person show you the color of their eyes? ....

10. If you order a **plain** hamburger, will it have mustard, mayonnaise, tomatoes, pickles, or onions on it? ....

See if you can write two more questions of your own using **two** of the remaining words in A.

11. ....

12. ....

Words that look alike #2 Which word

A. For each pair of similar-looking words taken from the **Oxford 3000**, circle *yes* or *no* to indicate whether you think the meanings of the two words are related or not. Be prepared to explain your answers.

chart¹ 🖉 **AWL** /tʃɑrt/ *noun* **1** [C] a drawing that shows information in the form of a diagram, etc.: *a temperature chart* ♦ *This chart shows the company's profits over the last three years.*

char·i·ty 🖉 /'tʃærəṭi/ *noun (pl.* **char·i·ties)** **1** [C, U] an organization that collects money to help people who are poor, sick, etc. or to do work that will be of benefit to society: *to raise money for charity* ♦ *He supports a charity that helps the handicapped.*

1.	**chart** (*noun*) – **charity**	yes	no	11.	**generate** – **generous**	yes	no
2.	**ad** – **advertisement**	yes	no	12.	**good** (*adjective*) – **goods**	yes	no
3.	**assist** – **assume**	yes	no	13.	**ill** (*adjective*) – **illegal**	yes	no
4.	**breath** – **breathe**	yes	no	14.	**mess** (*noun*) – **message**	yes	no
5.	**crime** – **criminal**	yes	no	15.	**pile** (*noun*) – **pilot** (*noun*)	yes	no
6.	**cope** – **copy** (*verb*)	yes	no	16.	**shallow** – **swallow** (*noun*)	yes	no
7.	**employer** – **employee**	yes	no	17.	**should** – **shoulder** (*noun*)	yes	no
8.	**fail** (*verb*) – **failure**	yes	no	18.	**solution** – **solve**	yes	no
9.	**feed** (*verb*) – **food**	yes	no	19.	**sum** (*verb*) – **summary** (*noun*)	yes	no
10.	**freeze** (*verb*) – **frozen**	yes	no	20.	**swell** (*verb*) – **swollen**	yes	no

B. Answer the questions in the space provided. If you need help, look up the **bold** words in your dictionary.

1. If you **assist** the police, does it make their task harder or easier? ....

2. Do you look at a **chart** for information or for entertainment? ....

3. Do you usually have to **cope** with something positive or negative? ....

4. Abigail donated $1,000, Brianna donated $25 and Christopher donated $1. Which one was the most **generous**? ....

5. Can you give three examples of manufactured **goods**? ....

6. If you make a **mess**, is this generally seen as a bad or a good thing? ....

7. A **pile** of crime, a **pile** of books, a **pile** of shoulders, a **pile** of charity – which one is the most likely? ....

8. Which is the correct combination? A **shallow** river or a **swallow** river? What is the opposite of your answer? ....

9. Is your **shoulder** above or below your waist? ....

10. Martha wrote a **summary** of a 10-page document. Was it 2 pages long or 12 pages long? ....

11. An **employer** or an **employee** – which one is the boss? ....

12. Which verb usually goes before the word *problems* – **breathe**, **solve**, or **swell**? ....

See if you can write two more questions of your own using **two** of the remaining words in A.

13. ....

14. ....

A. For each pair of similar-looking words taken from the **Oxford 3000**, circle *yes* or *no* to indicate whether you think the meanings of the two words are related or not. Be prepared to explain your answers.

> **guest** /gɛst/ *noun* [C] **1** a person that you invite to your home or to a particular event that you pay for: *We are having guests at our house this weekend.* ♦ *wedding guests* ♦ *an unexpected guest* ♦ *I went to the theater as Helen's guest.* ⊃ Look at **host**.

> **guess²** /gɛs/ *noun* [C] an attempt to give the right answer when you are not sure what it is: *If you don't know the answer, then take a guess!* ♦ *My guess is that they're stuck in traffic.* ♦ *Your guess is as good as mine* (= I don't know).

1.	**guess** (*noun*) – **guest**	yes	no	11.	**steep – step**	yes	no
2.	**drawer – drawing**	yes	no	12.	**adapt – adopt**	yes	no
3.	**urban – urgent**	yes	no	13.	**tendency - tension**	yes	no
4.	**former – formerly**	yes	no	14.	**cottage – cotton**	yes	no
5.	**deserve – preserve**	yes	no	15.	**wealth – weapon**	yes	no
6.	**stick** (*verb*) – **sticky**	yes	no	16.	**advice – advise**	yes	no
7.	**major – majority**	yes	no	17.	**pan – panel**	yes	no
8.	**promote – remote**	yes	no	18.	**emerge – emergency**	yes	no
9.	**hole – hollow** (*adjective*)	yes	no	19.	**identify – identity**	yes	no
10.	**inform – informal**	yes	no	20.	**seed – seek**	yes	no

B. Answer the questions in the space provided. If you need help, look up the **bold** words in your dictionary.

1. Is a **cottage** made of **cotton**? ....

2. Which of the following is <u>not</u> a **weapon** – a gun, a bomb, a helmet, or a dagger? ....

3. What was the name of the **former** eastern European country that included Serbia, Croatia, Slovenia, etc.?
....

4. If a student is **seek**ing the answer to a question, does she know the answer now? ....

5. Do you find many farms in **urban** neighborhoods? Explain your answer. ....

6. Staples, paper clips, and tape – you can use them all to attach two sheets of paper, but which of them is **sticky**? ....

7. A **drawer** (of a desk) and a **drawing** (of a person) are both related to the verb ***draw***, but the meaning of ***draw*** in each is different. Explain these two different meanings of the verb and say how they relate to the two nouns. ....

8. If an email is marked "**urgent**," what should you do? ....

9. If a tree is **hollow**, what does it have inside? ....

10. Which of these is a **remote** place to live – a high-rise in a busy downtown, a small farm in the countryside, or an apartment in a medium-size town? ....

11. Ryan has a **tendency** to talk too much when he's nervous. In your opinion, is that a good or a bad thing?
....

12. Who do people usually go to for legal **advice**? ....

See if you can write two more questions of your own using **two** of the remaining words in A.

13. ....

14. ....

Words that look alike #4 Which word

A. For each pair of similar-looking words taken from the **Oxford 3000**, circle *yes* or *no* to indicate whether you think the meanings of the two words are related or not. Be prepared to explain your answers.

bar·gain¹ /ˈbɑrɡən/ *noun* [C] **1** something that is cheaper or at a lower price than usual: *At that price, it's a real bargain!* ♦ *I found some good bargains at the garage sale.*

bar·ri·er /ˈbæriər/ *noun* [C] **1** an object that keeps people or things apart or prevents them from moving from one place to another: *The police put up barriers to stop the crowd from getting onto the road.*

1. **bargain** (*noun*) – **barrier**	yes	no	11. **quality – quantity**	yes no
2. **government – governor**	yes	no	12. **organ – origin**	yes no
3. **flash – flesh**	yes	no	13. **sail** (*verb*) – **sailor**	yes no
4. **pose** (*verb*) – **possess**	yes	no	14. **install – instance**	yes no
5. **soil – solid**	yes	no	15. **several – severely**	yes no
6. **vary – variety**	yes	no	16. **human – humorous**	yes no
7. **cure – curious**	yes	no	17. **star – stare**	yes no
8. **produce** (*verb*) – **product**	yes	no	18. **sign** (*verb*) – **signature**	yes no
9. **debt – debate** (*noun*)	yes	no	19. **opponent – oppose**	yes no
10. **arms – army**	yes	no	20. **strict – strike** (*verb*)	yes no

B. Answer the questions in the space provided. If you need help, look up the **bold** words in your dictionary.

1. If Jessica borrows $1,000 from Tyler and then $400 from David, how much is her total **debt**?

2. If you **stare** at a person, do they usually react positively or negatively?

3. Can you explain the different meanings of **strike** here? a.) The workers may **strike** again. b.) The enemy may **strike** again.

4. A sports car, a dangerous pet, a washing machine – which one do people **install**?

5. "There were **several** people waiting to go inside." Do you think there were 2, 5, or 20?

6. Use the Internet or your library to find out the **origin** of one of these English words: *algebra, denim, quarantine,* or *salary.*

7. On what type of vehicle do you usually find a **sailor**?

8. Name three **varieties** of colorful flowers.

9. Are people more likely to hold a **debate** on politics or on fashion?

10. If you pay $15,000 for a car that is worth $22,000, is the car a **bargain**?

11. If you **oppose** a candidate, are you likely to vote for that person in an upcoming election?

12. How can tiny toys **pose** a danger to young children?

See if you can write two more questions of your own using **two** of the remaining words in A.

13.

14.

A. For each pair of similar-looking words taken from the **Oxford 3000**, circle *yes* or *no* to indicate whether you think the meanings of the two words are related or not. Be prepared to explain your answers.

harm·ful 🔊 /ˈhɑrmfl/ *adj.* causing harm: *The new drug has no harmful side effects.* **ANT** **harmless**

harm·less 🔊 /ˈhɑrmləs/ *adj.* not able to cause harm; safe: *a harmless snake* **ANT** **harmful** ▶ **harm·less·ly** *adv.*

1.	**harmful – harmless**	yes	no	11.	**stand** (*verb*) – **standard**	yes	no
2.	**related – relatively**	yes	no	12.	**lawyer – layer**	yes	no
3.	**patience – pattern**	yes	no	13.	**substance – substitute**	yes	no
4.	**prove – provide**	yes	no	14.	**refuse** (*verb*) – **refusal**	yes	no
5.	**minimum** (*adjective*) – **minor** (*adjective*)	yes	no	15.	**stream** (*noun*) – **strength**	yes	no
6.	**entire – entitle**	yes	no	16.	**accompany – accommodation**	yes	no
7.	**local – location**	yes	no	17.	**sensible – sensitive**	yes	no
8.	**shall – shallow**	yes	no	18.	**table – tablet**	yes	no
9.	**pole – policy**	yes	no	19.	**appeal – appear**	yes	no
10.	**factor – factory**	yes	no	20.	**row** (*noun*) – **royal**	yes	no

B. Answer the questions in the space provided. If you need help, look up the **bold** words in your dictionary.

1. A ditch, a pond, a lake, an ocean – which of these is the **shallow**est? ....

2. How many **layers** does a birthday cake usually have? What about your last birthday cake? ....

3. Lauren can't **stand** the taste of broccoli. How often does she eat it? ....

4. If a steady **stream** of shoppers entered the store yesterday, did the store do good business that day? ....

5. I work from Monday to Friday. This week I had lunch with my coworker Alexis three days in a **row**. Alexis was out sick on Tuesday, so which days did we eat lunch together? ....

6. What do you think is the best **policy** about cell phones in class? ....

7. If the **entire** class of 20 students failed the exam, how many passed it? ....

8. AIDS, cancer, the flu – which of these three is **relatively minor**? ....

9. Which one of the following might you use as a **substitute** for sugar – honey, salt, or flour? Explain your answer. ....

10. Justin has a coupon that says "2 shirts for $20." How many shirts is he **entitled** to buy for $60? ....

11. Where might you find a **table** of contents? ....

12. John asked Olivia to marry him. Olivia **refused**. When are they getting married? ....

See if you can write two more questions of your own using **two** of the remaining words in A.

13. ....

14. ....

Spelling words correctly can be a challenge. There are spelling rules in English, but there are also many exceptions. Additionally, English has many silent letters and double consonants. Your dictionary is an extremely valuable resource for verifying the correct spelling of a word.

comb¹ /koʊm/ *noun* [C] a piece of metal or plastic with a row of teeth that you use for making your hair neat

comb

nap² /næp/ *verb* [I] (**nap·ping**, **napped**) to have a short sleep

A. Find the silent letter in each of the following words.

dou___t	forei___n	su___tle	lis___en
ca___m	cas___le	mus___le	___nife

B. Write the correct spelling of any misspelled words in this list. Some words are correct.

1. occured ....
2. persaverance ....
3. harass ....
4. occurrence ....
5. pasttime ....
6. millenium ....
7. responsable ....
8. priviledge ....
9. weird ....
10. definately ....
11. campain ....
12. accommodate ....
13. mispell ....
14. embarrassment ....
15. grammer ....
16. seperate ....
17. believe ....
18. colum ....

C. Fill in the blanks in the following sentences with the correct spelling of a word from Part B.

1. A van can .... more passengers than a car.
2. The loss of electricity .... just after midnight.
3. My favorite .... is collecting coins from different countries.
4. Please write your answers in the left ....
5. Wow! The temperature today is .... colder than it was yesterday.
6. A teacher must know a lot about English ....
7. People often .... the word "parallel".
8. At that restaurant, there is a .... menu for desserts.
9. With a great deal of ...., I know you can improve your English.
10. It is a great .... to be working with Dr. Wilkins.

A compound is a word or phrase that consists of two or more parts that combine to express a single meaning. They can be spelled as one word (like **firefighter**), two or more separate words (like **coffee table**), or with a hyphen (like **hard-working** and **double-park**).

> ,hard-'working (also hard·work·ing) *adj.*
> working with effort and energy: *a hard-working student*

> 'coffee ,table *noun* [C] a low table, usually in a living room

> ,double-'park *verb* [I, T] (usually passive) to park a car beside another car that is already parked at the side of the street: *I'll have to rush – I'm double-parked.*

A. Match a word from the left-hand column with a word in the right-hand column to make a compound. Notice if it is spelled with or without a hyphen (-) and what part of speech it is (noun or adjective).

lamp	tide	lampshade	noun
long	year		
life	back		
locker	guard		
left	shade		
low	term		
leap	room		
laid	handed		

In general, compound adjectives and verbs tend to have a hyphen, while nouns do not.

B. Answer the questions about the compound words. Use your dictionary to find the meaning of any compounds that you cannot figure out.

1. For an author, is a **best-selling** book a good thing? ....
2. Can you buy a stove at a **bake sale**? ....
3. Is a **bald eagle** bald? ....
4. Are you a **couch potato**? ....
5. Which is cheaper – cheap or **dirt cheap**? ....
6. If a race ends in a **dead heat**, does it mean that the temperature is high? ....
7. A rare five-cent stamp from 1937 is now worth $8,000. What is its **face value**? ....
8. Is a **high-rise** a person or a thing? ....
9. Which month is affected in a **leap year**? ....
10. Can you name a **make-believe** person? ....
11. What kind of food can be cooked **sunny-side up**? ....
12. When people go **window shopping**, what kind of windows do they usually buy? ....

See if you can write two more questions of your own using **two** of the following compounds.

emergency room	doggy bag	old-fashioned	high five	brainwash

13. ....
14. ....

C. Some of these compound words are easier to understand than others. For example, **hard-working** is easy: You can *work hard*. However, a **coffee table** often has magazines on it more often than it has a coffee on it. In your opinion, which of these compounds in this lesson are the most difficult to understand?

....
....
....

As we saw in Lesson 13, compound adjectives and verbs are often spelled with a hyphen, and nouns without one. There are, however, many exceptions so it is better to look up compounds in your dictionary to make sure that you spell them correctly .

bulletin ,board *noun* [C] a board on a wall for putting papers, signs, etc. on

entry- level *adj.* (**BUSINESS**) (of a job) at the lowest level in a company: *an entry-level job*

A. Add a hyphen to the words in the first column that are missing hyphens. Then read the statements about the compound words and write TRUE or FALSE in the Answer column next to each statement. Use your dictionary to check the spelling and meaning of any compound words that you do not know well.

	Spelling in context: hyphen or not?	Meaning: true or false?	Answer
1.	He's a **warm-hearted** guy.	He's a nice guy.	true
2.	The police called the driver's **next of kin**.	The police called the driver's family.	
3.	A **record breaking** audience watched the game last night.	It was a usual size for the audience.	
4.	She wrote her name in **block letters**.	She wrote "Susan Juffs."	
5.	Tim is my **brother in law**.	Tim is my wife's husband.	
6.	Paula is a **sought after** singer.	Paula is a very popular singer.	
7.	We watched the **ball game** on TV.	It was probably a basketball game.	
8.	Luke was the **runner up** in the race.	Luke finished last in the race.	
9.	The news was **earth shattering** to me.	I was not interested in the news.	
10.	Wendy has the **know how** for this job.	Wendy is qualified for this job.	
11.	Karen **cross examined** the man.	Karen might be a lawyer.	
12.	The teacher gave a **pop quiz**.	The students knew about the test.	

B.

1. Use the words from the Word Bank to complete these compound words. Pay attention to the hyphens or lack of hyphens.

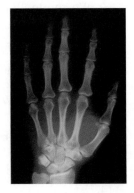

WORD BANK

friendly   voice   load   pass   trip   lay   ray   check   plastic

1. a boarding...
2. to down...
3. ....mail
4. a ....over
5. a round...ticket

6. ....surgery
7. a ....up
8. user...
9. an X...

2. Place the 9 compounds from the previous exercise in the right subject area. You can check the meanings in your dictionary.

travel	health	computing

English uses a lot of short forms and abbreviations, some of them just in writing and others in speech as well. Your dictionary will tell you what word or words the abbreviations stand for, and will also show you if a word has a commonly-used abbreviation.

For example, you may read that someone was " taken to the ER". Look up the entry for **ER** (between **equivalent** and **era**) and you will find that the full form is EMERGENCY ROOM. The entry for **emergency room** tells you what it means and also contains the abbreviation **ER**.

> e'mergency ,room *noun* [C] (*abbr.* ER) (**HEALTH**)
> the part of a hospital where people who need urgent treatment are taken: *He was rushed to the emergency room.*
> **ER** /ˌiˈɑr/ *abbr.* = EMERGENCY ROOM

Use the across and down clues to complete this crossword puzzle. If you need help, look at the entry for the abbreviation or the full form in your dictionary.

HINT If the abbreviation is given with a period (.), you don't need to write that in the puzzle.

8 across

13 across

19 down

21 down

Across clues

1. Full form of the word that is the opposite of Jr.
6. PR stands for .... relations
8. An unidentified flying object
9. Abbreviation of curriculum vitae
10. The A in A.D. (used in dates) stands for ....
12. Abbreviation for the eighth month of the year
13. A registered nurse is an ....
14. Tuberculosis is often called ....
15. The abbreviation for trademark
16. An .... card is an identification card
19. A title for an adult male, as in "Good morning, ... Garcia."
20. A direction: E
21. lb., oz. and kg. are measures of ....
24. A country that borders Canada and Mexico
26. 1/16 of 1 lb.
27. The opposite direction from 20 across

Down clues

2. IT = ... Technology
3. Five cubic feet = 5 .... ft.
4. Abbreviation for a wide street in a city, for example, *Sunset* ....
5. The full name of the month before Nov.
6. A measure of weight equal to 16 oz.
7. Before Christ (used for years)
8. The United Nations is commonly called the ....
11. A direction: northeast
17. Bachelor of Arts degree
18. Abbreviation for sergeant
19. Abbreviation for mount or mountain, as in .... *Fuji*
20. An extension of a telephone line
21. WWW = World .... Web
22. A teaching assistant is a ....
23. The opposite direction from 11 down
24. A different abbreviation for 24 across
25. Abbreviation for street, as in 220 *Jefferson* ....

Sometimes it is not easy to pronounce a new English word because one letter can have different sounds (**a** in *about* or *able*), some letters are silent (**e** in *cake* or **b** in *crumb*), and two letters can combine to make a different sound (**ph** in *phone* or **gh** in *tough*). The full guide to phonetic spellings is found on the inside front cover of your **Oxford American Dictionary** and the following symbols are given at the bottom of the pages.

æ cat	ɛ ten	i see	ɪ sit	ɑ hot	ɔ saw	ʌ cup	ʊ put	u too
ə about	y yes	w woman	t̬ butter	eɪ say	aɪ five	ɔɪ boy	aʊ now	oʊ go
ər bird	ɪr near	ɛr hair	ɑr car	ɔr north	ʊr tour	ʒ vision	h hat	ŋ sing
tʃ chin	dʒ June	v van	θ thin	ð then	s so	z zoo	ʃ she	

A. Complete the following sentences with the correct answers from the Word Bank. Write your answers using the phonetic spellings. You only need to use **five** of the seven words.

WORD BANK

> **June   aunt   coat   dozen   monkey   seven   green**

1. /maɪ ˈfeɪvrət ˈkʌlər ɪz/   /.........................../.
2. /ɪf ðə ˈwɛðər ɪz koʊld yu kæn wɛr ə/   /.........................../.
3. /ðə mʌnθ bɪˈfɔr dʒuˈlaɪ ɪz/   /.........................../.
4. /yər ˈmʌðərz ˈsɪstər ɪz yər/   /.........................../.
5. /ə wərd ðət minz ə grup əv twɛlv ɪz/   /.........................../.

B. The following groups of three words have similar pronunciations. Choose which phonetic spelling corresponds to the meaning given and write the other words. Use your dictionary to check the spellings.

	Pronunciations	Meaning	Correct word	The other words are ...
1.	a. /kɛr/ b. /ʃɛr/ c. /tʃɛr/	a piece of furniture for one person to sit on	c. chair	care, share
2.	a. /bæt/ b. /pæt/ c. /væt/	a gentle tap with a flat hand		
3.	a. /kʌb/ b. /kʌp/ c. /kʌf/	a container used for drinking liquids		
4.	a. /ʃɛl/ b. /dʒɛl/ c. /hɛl/	a thick substance like jelly that is between a liquid and a solid		
5.	a. /laɪt/ b. /raɪt/ c. /raɪd/	pale; not dark		
6.	a. /lif/ b. /lip/ c. /lɪp/	a big jump		
7.	a. /ʃaɪ/ b. /θaɪ/ c. /taɪ/	something that you wear around your neck		
8.	a. /θɪk/ b. /sɪk/ c. /sik/	not thin		
9.	a. /sɪp/ b. /ʃɪp/ c. /ʃip/	a large boat		
10.	a. /hɑt/ b. /hæt/ c. /haɪt/	a high place or area		

C. Which words are difficult for you to pronounce? Find **five** words in your dictionary that are difficult for you to pronounce. Write those five words and the pronunciation here. Compare answers with other students in your class.

Word	Pronunciation
1.	/..................... /
2.	/..................... /
3.	/..................... /
4.	/..................... /
5.	/..................... /

Stress in two-syllable words Part 1 Pronunciation

A word consists of one or more syllables. Words of two or more syllables have one syllable that is stressed, or emphasized, more than the other(s). Knowing which syllable to stress is extremely important – if you stress the wrong syllable, it can make your English difficult to understand.

> **pal·ace** 🔊 /'pæləs/ *noun* [C] a large house that is or was the home of a king or queen

There are some general rules for stressing two-syllable words, but there are many exceptions that you may need to look up in your dictionary. In the **Oxford American Dictionary**, the syllable with the main stress has a **primary stress** mark (') in front of that syllable.

A.

1. Look at the following list of common two-syllable words. Decide what part of speech they are (*nouns*, *verbs*, or *adjectives*) and which syllable is stressed, the first or the second. You can use your dictionary to check.

Word	Part of speech	Stressed syllable
palace	*noun*	*first*
planet		
pleasant		
possess		
pronounce		
painter		

Word	Part of speech	Stressed syllable
painful		
passport		
prefer		
partner		
perform		
publish		

2. Now underline the correct words in this statement:

"Based on this sample, most two-syllable (*adjectives/nouns/verbs*) and (*adjectives/nouns/verbs*) stress the first syllable, and many two-syllable (*adjectives/nouns/verbs*) stress the second syllable."

ⓘ For another useful rule see the foot of this page.

B.
Read these groups of **six** words containing two syllables. In each group, circle the word that has a different stress pattern than the other five words. Use your dictionary to check any pronunciations that you are not sure of.

1. baggage cellphone honest occur tourist website
2. convince deserve install meeting provide until
3. nonsense number silence summer today traffic
4. although decay derive mention replace withdraw
5. region retired rival spider sticky surname
6. attached beyond confined decide forecast observe
7. happen narrow railroad naked rightly unique
8. balance cancer daughter highlight survive victim

C.
Look up the eight words you circled in your dictionary from sentences 1–8. They are all from the **Oxford 3000** list of common words that you need to know. Choose the best one to fit in each of the sentences below and then read the sentence out loud.

1. Mike is a .... teacher.
2. The koala is .... to Australia.
3. Many birds did not .... the harsh winter.
4. When did the accident ....?
5. Our next .... is on February 10.
6. Rain is .... for this afternoon.
7. Just don't .... Eric in front of her!
8. In math class ...., we had a pop quiz.

* "When the endings -*er*, -*est*, -*ful*, -*ing*, -*less*, -*ly*, -*ment*, -*ness*, -*ship* or –*tion* create a two-syllable word, the first syllable is stressed."

Stress in two-syllable words Part 2 Pronunciation

Did you know that there are more two-syllable words in the **Oxford 3000** list of keywords than any other group? This shows how common two-syllable words are in English, and why it is important to practice their pronunciation as much as possible.

The stress in a two-syllable word may depend on the word's part of speech. Sometimes when a word functions as both noun and verb, the first syllable is stressed when it is a noun, but the second syllable is stressed when it is a verb. Consider the two entries for the word **object** from your **Oxford American Dictionary**.

> **ob·ject¹** 🔊 /ˈɑbdʒɛkt; -dʒɪkt/ *noun* [C] **1** a thing that can be seen and touched, but is not alive: *The shelves were filled with objects of all shapes and sizes.* ◆
> **ob·ject²** 🔊 /əbˈdʒɛkt/ *verb* **1** [I] **object (to sb/sth)** to not like or to be against someone or something:

A. Each pair of sentences has two uses of one word. In each case underline the stressed syllable. Consult your dictionary if you need help. The first one has been done for you.

1. They decided to **conduct** an experiment to test their theory. The experiment affected the rats' **conduct**.
2. Who won the talent **contest**? Both of you can **contest** the result.
3. We **import** most of our oil from Canada. Copper is a major **import** into China.
4. Their action was an **insult** to us. They often **insult** people.
5. I **object** to what he said. That's an unusual **object** to find in a museum.
6. You need to obtain a **permit** from the city. Some parents won't **permit** their children to eat candy.
7. These six large farms **produce** 90% of our food. Farmers' markets sell mainly local **produce**.
8. Teenagers often **rebel** against authority. I am considered a **rebel** in my family.
9. The county clerk will **record** the birth. There is an official **record** of her birth in 1893.

B. Practice reading aloud these sentences that include underlined two-syllable words. Write a 1 or 2 above the word to indicate which syllable is stressed. Use your dictionary to check any pronunciations that you are not sure of.

1. The <u>author</u> <u>received</u> a <u>rather</u> large <u>amount</u> of <u>money</u> as a <u>birthday</u> <u>present</u> from her <u>partner</u>.

2. The <u>suspect's</u> <u>reply</u> to the <u>police</u> officer's <u>questions</u> <u>amazed</u> them, but that was his <u>object</u>.

3. In this <u>instance</u>, we all <u>agree</u> that <u>hatred</u> is not a <u>healthy</u> <u>feeling</u> that <u>people</u> can just <u>ignore</u>.

4. The <u>extreme</u> cold <u>weather</u> this <u>April</u> may <u>result</u> in <u>damage</u> to both <u>garden</u> and <u>forest</u> plants.

5. <u>Parents</u> and <u>teachers</u> <u>sometimes</u> <u>demand</u> that <u>children</u> <u>study</u> <u>subjects</u> they don't <u>enjoy</u>.

C. Place names

Circle 1 or 2 to indicate where the stress is. Consult the list of geographical names in your dictionary (on pages R16–R20) if you need help.

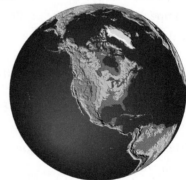

1 2	1 2	1 2	1 2
Brazil	Japan	Sweden	Turkey
1 2	1 2	1 2	1 2
China	Kenya	Peru	Jordan
1 2	1 2	1 2	1 2
Egypt	Thailand	Kuwait	Iceland
1 2	1 2	1 2	1 2
Chile	Iraq	Iran	Norway

Frequent words with the letters "ou" Pronunciation

In English, spelling and pronunciation do not match 100%. A common vowel combination is *ou*. The letters *ou* have at least six different pronunciations. Study the following examples:

Word	Phonetic transcription	*ou* is pronounced...	Rhymes with...
cloud	/klaʊd/	/aʊ/	now (This is the most common pronunciation.)
soup	/sup/	/u/	too
cough	/kɔf/	/ɔ/	saw
young	/yʌŋ/	/ʌ/	cup
though	/ðoʊ/	/oʊ/	go
should	/ʃʊd/	/ʊ/	put (This is just *could*, *should*, and *would*.)

cloud¹ /klaʊd/ *noun* **1** [C, U] a small drops of water that floats in often grey or white: *The sun disapp...*

soup¹ /sup/ *noun* [U] liquid foo cooking meat, vegetables, etc. in ... of soup

A. Read these groups of **three** words containing the letters *ou*. Circle the word that has a different pronunciation for *ou* than the other two words. Use your **Oxford American Dictionary** to check any pronunciations that you are not sure of.

1. account   could   shout
2. loud   south   youth
3. although   rough   trouble
4. doubt   group   wounded
5. ground   ought   sound
6. aloud   shoulder   soul
7. country   couple   proud
8. amount   bound   routine
9. cough   thought   through
10. though   touch   tough
11. mount   out   soup
12. mouse   round   should

B. Place these eighteen words containing the letters *ou* under the headword that has the same pronunciation for *ou*. Use your dictionary to check any pronunciations that you are not sure of.

although	could	encounter	proud	routine	shout	thought	tough	wounded
amount	cousin	ought	rough	shoulder	soul	through	would	youth

cloud	soup	cough	young	though	should
1.	1.	1.	1.	1.	1.
2.	2.	2.	2.	2.	2.
3.	3.		3.	3.	
4.	4.				

C. All of the words in this unit are from the **Oxford 3000** list of common words that you should know. Consult your **Oxford American Dictionary** and use this space to write any information for **four** words containing *ou* that you do not know well.

Word	Meaning(s)	Example(s)
bound	1 certain to do something 2 traveling or leading to a particular place	*You're bound to get an A on the test.* *a ship bound for Australia* *the southbound lanes of the freeway*
1.		
2.		
3.		
4.		

A noun is the name of a person, place, thing, or idea. In your dictionary, these important words are marked with the label *noun* just after them.

Some nouns are related to other parts of speech (such as verbs or adjectives) and have endings, such as –tion (**explanation**), -er (**driver**), -ness (**happiness**), or –ment (**enjoyment**). Other nouns have the same form as their related verb (**cough**) or adjective (**gray**).

If you know the verb or the adjective you can find the related noun in your dictionary in one of four ways:

(1) It is the same word as the verb or adjective but has a separate entry with a small number next to it.

> **cough¹** /kɔf/ *verb* [I] (**HEALTH**) to send air out of your throat and mouth with a sudden loud noise, especially when you have a cold, have something

> **cough²** (**HEALTH**) /kɔf/ *noun* [C] **1** an act or the sound of coughing: *He gave a nervous cough before he started to speak.* **2** an illness or infection that makes

(2) It has a separate entry which is usually nearby.

(3) It is a derivative at the end of the verb or adjective entry.

> **lone·ly** /ˈloʊnli/ *adj.* (**lone·li·er, lone·li·est**)
> **1** unhappy because you are not with other people: *to feel sad and lonely* **2** (only *before* a noun) far from other people and places where people live: *a lonely house in the hills* ⊃ Look at the note at **alone**. ▶ **lone·li·ness** *noun* [U]

(4) It is given as a cross reference after an arrow symbol.

> **mar·ry** /ˈmæri/ *verb* (pres. part. **mar·ry·ing**, 3rd person sing. pres. **mar·ries**, pt., pp. **mar·ried**) **1** [I, T] to take someone as your husband or wife: *They married when they were very young.* ◆ *When did Roger ask you to marry him?*
> **2** [T] to join two people together as husband and wife: *We asked John's priest to marry us.* ⊃ noun **marriage**

A. Write the noun related to the following verbs and adjectives.

1. **locate** ....
2. **adhere** ....
3. **restore** ....
4. **greet** ....
5. **deny** ....
6. **approach** (*verb*) ....
7. **adopt** ....
8. **detain** ....
9. **cruel** ....
10. **imply** ....
11. **extravagant** ....
12. **complain** ....
13. **classic** (*adj.*) ....
14. **secure** ....
15. **brief** (*adj.*) ....
16. **ventilate** ....

B. Complete these sentences with the noun that is related to the word in **bold**. Your dictionary can help you in the ways listed above.

1. If you **gesture** for the waiter to come to your table, what kind of .... do you use?
2. If you **replace** your current car, what kind of .... will you get?
3. If you want to **repel** mosquitoes, you can use insect ....
4. If the pool is six feet **deep**, it has a .... of six feet.
5. If you **add** a room to your house, it is an ....
6. Some people cannot **decide** anything. They find it difficult to make a ....
7. Even when all the weather reports **forecast** bad weather, the .... can be wrong.
8. To **display** their merchandise and increase sales, a business can set up a .... of their products.
9. If you **gossip** about someone, you are spreading .... about that person.
10. If an author is **interesting** to you, you have an .... in her work.
11. Before a wedding, there is usually a .... where they **rehearse** everything.
12. Not having your own car can be a real .... when looking for a new job because it **hinders** your chances of employment.

Nouns (multiple meanings) Parts of speech

One noun can often have two or more meanings. For example, the word **calf** can mean the back of your leg or a young cow.

calf /kæf/ *noun* [C] (*pl.* **calves** /kævz/) **1** the back of your leg, below your knee ➜ See picture at **body**. **2** a young cow ➜ Look at the note at **cow**.

A. Match each of the following six nouns with <u>two</u> different definitions.

.... an **issue**   .... a **lap**   .... a **log**

.... a **minority**   .... a **quarter**   .... a **race**

1. = 15 minutes
2. = a thick piece of wood that is cut from or has fallen from a tree
3. = one trip around a race track, across a pool, etc.
4. = an official written record of something, written over a period of time
5. = one of the groups into which people can be divided according to the color of their skin, their hair type, the shape of their face, etc.
6. = one in a series of things that are published or produced
7. = a competition between people, animals, cars, etc., to see which is the fastest
8. = the flat area that is formed by the upper part of your legs when you are sitting down
9. = 25 cents
10. = a group of people who are of a different race or religion from most of the people in the country where they live
11. = a problem or subject for discussion
12. = the smaller number or part of a group; less than half

B. Use the words in the Word Bank to fill the gaps in the following phrases. Each word is used twice. Next to each one, write the number of that meaning in your dictionary.

WORD BANK

| bridge   chain   course   pack   press   story |

	Phrase	Meaning number
1.	a golf	
2.	a .... over the river	
3.	a .... in intermediate Spanish	
4.	a .... of chewing gum	
5.	a printing	
6.	a fifty-................. building	
7.	a .... of restaurants	
8.	a .... of wolves	
9.	the .... of a bicycle	
10.	the freedom of the	
11.	the .... of Cinderella	
12.	a game of	

C. Now see if you can write some short phrases of your own using **two** different senses of each of the following three nouns.

| anchor   block   volume |

1. ....   4. ....

2. ....   5. ....

3. ....   6. ....

Verbs (word families) Parts of speech

A verb is a word that is used to indicate an action or a state. In your dictionary, these important words are marked with the label *verb* just after them.

Some verbs are related to other parts of speech (such as nouns or adjectives) and have endings, such as –ize (**symbolize**), -en (**widen**) or -ify (**simplify**). Some verbs have the same form as their related noun (**sneeze**) or adjective (**clean**).

If you know the noun or the adjective, you can find the related verb in your dictionary in one of four ways:

(1) It is the same word as the noun or adjective but has a separate entry with a small number next to it.

(2) It has a separate entry which is usually nearby.

(3) It is a derivative at the end of the verb or adjective entry.

> **sum·ma·ry¹** 🔊 **AWL** /'sʌməri/ *noun* [C] (*pl.* **sum-ma·ries**) a short description of the main ideas or events of something: *A brief summary of the experiment is given at the beginning of the report.* ♦ *a news summary* ▶ **sum·ma·rize** **AWL** /'sʌməraɪz/ *verb* [T]: *Could you summarize the story so far?*

(4) It is given as a cross reference after an arrow symbol.

> **per·cep·tion** **AWL** /pər'sɛpʃn/ *noun* **1** [U] the ability to notice or understand something **2** [C] a particular way of looking at or understanding something; an opinion: *What is your perception of the situation?* ➲ verb **perceive**

A. Write the verb related to the following words.

1. an **interruption** ....
2. a **broadcast** ....
3. an **offense** ....
4. a **warning** ....
5. a **cut** ....
6. **stress** ....
7. **stable** (*adj.*) ....
8. **emphasis** ....
9. **proof** ....
10. a **picnic** ....
11. **reliable** ....
12. **diverse** ....
13. a **burglar** ....
14. **conception** ....
15. a **map** ....
16. a **massage** ....

B. Irregular verbs do not add –ed to form the past tense. Irregular forms for verbs are listed with the symbol *pt.* (= past tense) and the form. Write the past tense of these irregular verbs.

> **sweep¹** 🔊 /swip/ *verb* (*pt., pp.* **swept** /swɛpt/)
> **1** [I, T] to clean a room, surface, etc. using a brush with a long handle (a **broom**): *Could you sweep under the table too?* ♦ *Take your shoes off! I just swept the floor.*

1. **get** ....
2. **fall** ....
3. **quit** ....
4. **wake** ....
5. **flee** ....
6. **set** ....
7. **beat** ....
8. **sink** ....
9. **throw** ....
10. **let** ....
11. **spin** ....
12. **lead** ....
13. **forgive** ....
14. **grow** ....
15. **dig** ....
16. **burst** ....
17. **spread** ....
18. **wind up** ....

C. Complete these sentences with the verb that is related to the word in **bold**. Your dictionary can help you in the ways listed above.

1. This rice lacks **flavor**. You can .... it by adding butter or salt.
2. Our team didn't .... any points at all, so the final **score** was 7-0.
3. The **abbreviation** for January is Jan., so how do you .... February and March?
4. She threatened to sue him for **slander** so that he wouldn't .... her anymore.
5. At a teachers' **conference**, I can .... with other teachers.
6. To get a **refund**, present your receipt within a week and ask the clerk to .... your money.
7. The bank issued a **denial** in its attempt to .... any involvement in the scandal.

Verbs (multiple meanings) Parts of speech

One verb can often have two or more meanings. For example, **stand** can mean to be on your feet or, in negative sentences, to dislike.

stand¹ /stænd/ *verb* [I, T] (*pt.*, *pp.* **stood** /stʊd/)
> **ON FEET/UPRIGHT 1** [I] to be on your feet; to be in a vertical position: *He was standing near the window.* ◆ *Stand still – I'm trying to take a photo of you.*

> **DISLIKE 9** [T] (in negative sentences and questions, with *can/could*) used to emphasize that you do not like someone or something: *I can't stand that obnoxious guy on the local radio.* ◆ *How can you stand it when she practices her trumpet?*

A. Match each of the following six verbs with <u>two</u> different definitions.

.... **settle**   .... **issue**   .... **practice**   .... **ground**   .... **launch**   .... **back**

1. = to send a ship into water or a space vehicle into the sky
2. = to force an aircraft to stay on the ground
3. = to do something many times to become good at it
4. = to start something new
5. = to choose a permanent home
6. = to make something known to the public
7. = to supply something to someone
8. = to give help or suppport to someone
9. = to work as a doctor or lawyer
10. = to end an argument
11. = to move backward
12. = to punish a child by not allowing him or her to leave the house

B. Use the words in the Word Bank to fill the gaps in the following phrases. Each word is used twice. Next to each one, write the number of that meaning in your dictionary.

WORD BANK

beam   bolt   hold   land   miss   pick

	Phrase	Meaning number
1.	When I was in China, I ....ed my family a lot.	
2.	Our flight will .... at noon.	
3.	I always .... my front door before going to bed.	
4.	She was ....ing the baby in her arms.	
5.	The program was ....ed to more than 50 nations.	
6.	I need to .... my classes for next semester.	
7.	The farmers are going to .... their apples soon.	
8.	The horse ....ed when it heard the thunder.	
9.	I ....ed two shots in the last basketball game.	
10.	They are planning to .... a party for Joshua in August.	
11.	I hope I can .... a better job really soon.	
12.	After he got the new job, he was ....ing with delight.	

C. Now see if you can write some short phrases of your own using **two** different senses of each of the following three verbs.

fire   push   turn

1. ....
2. ....
3. ....

4. ....
5. ....
6. ....

Adjectives (word families) Parts of speech

An adjective is a word that tells you more about a noun (or pronoun). In your dictionary, these important words are marked with the label *adj.* just after them.

Some adjectives are related to other parts of speech (nouns or verbs) and have endings, such as –y (**sunny**), -ing (**annoying**), -ent (**different**), -al (**national**), –ful (**beautiful**), or –ern (**southern**).

Some nouns can be used like adjectives without any special endings: we say "a **city** election" but "a **national** election" (not nation).

If you know the noun or verb, you can find the related adjective in your dictionary in one of four ways:

(1) It is the same word as the noun or verb but has a separate entry with a small number next to it.

(2) It has a separate entry which is usually nearby.

(3) It is a derivative at the end of noun or verb entry.

> **ev·o·lu·tion** AWL /ˌɛvəˈluʃn/ *noun* [U] **1** (BIOLOGY) the development of plants, animals, etc. over many thousands of years from simple early forms to more advanced ones: *Darwin's theory of evolution* **2** the process of change and development: *Political evolution is a slow process.* ▶ **ev·o·lu·tionary** AWL /ˌɛvəˈluʃəˌnɛri/ *adj.*: *evolutionary theory*

(4) It is given as a cross reference after an arrow symbol.

> **en·vy**[1] /ˈɛnvi/ *noun* [U] **envy (of sb/sth)** the feeling that you have when someone else has something that you want: *It was difficult for her to hide her envy of her friend's success.* **SYN** **jealousy** ⊃ adjective **envious**

A. Write the adjective related to the following words.

1. **addition**	....	9. **escape**	....
2. **fury**	....	10. **help**	....
3. **success**	....	11. **wonder**	....
4. **shock**	....	12. **fur**	....
5. **logic**	....	13. **rain**	....
6. **entertain**	....	14. **flaw**	....
7. **curl**	....	15. **power**	....
8. **emotion**	....	16. **interest**	.... and ....

B. Participle adjectives end in –ed or –ing. In general, we use –ed for a person or thing that is receiving the feeling of the adjective, and –ing for the person or thing that is causing the feeling of the adjective. Add –ed or –ing to complete the adjectives in these sentences.

> **an·noyed** /əˈnɔɪd/ *adj.* feeling angry or slightly angry: *He's annoyed that no one believes him.* ♦ *I was annoyed to see that they had left the door open.* ♦ *She's annoyed at herself for making such a stupid mistake.*
> **an·noy·ing** /əˈnɔɪɪŋ/ *adj.* making you feel angry or slightly angry: *That constant hammering noise is really annoying.*

1. My neighbor's dog barks constantly, which I find really **annoy**............ .
2. Kim comes from a rather **isolat**............ region of his country.
3. According to the report, we may experience **damag**............ winds tonight.
4. The cost of gasoline is soaring at an **alarm**............ rate.
5. I couldn't follow the teacher's explanation and left the class quite **confus**............ .
6. When Christopher discovered he had failed the test, he was **embarrass**............ .
7. Though it lost money last year, the company's most recent business report contained very **promis**............ data.
8. The only way we could keep Chelsea **amus**............ was to take her to the zoo.
9. Our loss to our biggest rival was a **humiliat**............ experience.
10. By the end of the first class meeting, I was already **concern**............ about the amount of work.
11. A **surpris**............ number of people complained about last night's broadcast.
12. In history class, I am always so **bor**............ .

Adverbs (word families) Parts of speech

An adverb is a word that adds information to a verb, adjective, phrase, or another adverb. In your dictionary, these important words are marked with the label *adv.* just after them.

The majority of adverbs in English are related to adjectives and end in –ly (**angrily, differently, honestly**).

If you know the adjective, you can find the related adverb in your dictionary in one of three ways:

(1) It is a derivative at the end of the adjective entry.

> **cheer·ful** 🖉 /'tʃɪrfl/ *adj.* happy: *Tom seems very cheerful despite his illness.* ◆ *a cheerful smile* ▶ **cheer-ful·ly** *adv.*

(2) It has a separate entry which is usually nearby.

(3) It is the same word as the adjective but has a separate entry with a small number next to it.

> **hard¹** 🖉 /hɑrd/ *adj.*
> ▸ SOLID/STIFF **1** not soft to touch; not easy to break or bend; very firm: *The bed was so hard that I couldn't*

> **hard²** 🖉 /hɑrd/ *adv.* **1** with great effort, energy, or attention: *He worked hard all his life.* ◆ *You'll have to try*

Note that many adverbs do not end in –ly (for example, **therefore, yesterday, upstairs**). In addition, some -ly words are adjectives (**friendly, lonely**). The only way to know that these words are adverbs is to note their usage in context or consult your dictionary.

A. Write the adverb related to the following words.

1. **voluntary** ....
2. **serious** ....
3. **inevitable** ....
4. **random** ....
5. **visual** ....
6. **arbitrary** ....
7. **automatic** ....
8. **bitter** ....
9. **easy** ....
10. **dramatic** ....
11. **likely** ....
12. **immediate** ....
13. **predominant** ....
14. **fast** ....
15. **radical** ....
16. **proper** ....

B. Select the **two** correct adverbs from the six in each sentence.

1. (Broadly, Perfectly, Unfortunately), in today's game, Daniel and Joshua played (absolutely, deeply, nervously) and did not score any points.
2. Mohammed is (originally, permanently, sufficiently) from Egypt, but he now speaks English (desperately, fluently, ultimately).
3. In the morning, it was raining (efficiently, lightly, stiffly), but it (carelessly, gradually, heavily) ceased by noon.
4. Emma and Abigail (deliberately, softly, tightly) sat together in the library so they could (equally, morally, quietly) compare class notes.
5. Sophia is (nearly, personally, substantially) older than her sister Mia, but Mia is (normally, practically, steeply) the same height.

C. Study carefully the dictionary definitions of these four adverbs: **hard, hardly, late, lately**. Then underline the correct adverb in these sentences.

1. (Hard / Hardly) any passengers fly in first class due to the high fare.
2. Passengers who arrive at the airport (late / lately) may be denied boarding.
3. (Late / Lately) Tyler has not been studying very (hard / hardly).
4. Megan (hard / hardly) does any homework and usually comes to class (late / lately).
5. I used to see Olivia a lot, but I've (hard / hardly) seen her (late / lately).

A preposition is a word or phrase that is used before a noun or pronoun to show place, time, direction, etc. Prepositions are usually small words, such as **at**, **in**, **on**, **by**, **with**, **for**, **to**, with a few longer ones such as **before**, **after**, and **according to**. In your dictionary, these important words are marked with the label *prep.* just after them.

Using the correct preposition is one of the most difficult aspects of English. The choice of which preposition to use is usually determined by the noun that comes after it. For example, a book can be **on** the table or **in** the drawer. A test can be **on** Monday or **in** May.

At other times, however, the choice of the preposition is determined by the word that comes before it, which can be a noun (the **reason for** something), adjective (I'm **interested in** something), or verb (we **accuse** someone **of** something).

You can find the correct preposition usage in your dictionary by studying the example sentences or by studying the phrase in **bold print** that comes just before the meaning.

> **on** /ɑn; ɔn/ *adv.*, *prep.* **1** supported by a surface: *The plates are on the table.* ◆ *We sat on the floor.*

> **6** with expressions of time: *on August 19th* ◆ *on Monday* ◆ *on Thanksgiving* ◆ *What are you doing on your birthday?* **7** immediately

> **in¹** /ɪn/ *adv.*, *prep.* **1** (used to show place) inside or to a position within a particular area or object: *a country in Africa* ◆ *an island in the Pacific* ◆ *in a box* ◆ *I read about it in the newspaper.* ◆ *He lay in bed.*

> **3** (showing time) during a period of time: *My birthday is in August.* ◆ *He was born in 1995.* ◆ *You could walk there in about an hour* (= it would take that long to walk there).

> **ac·cuse** /əˈkyuz/ *verb* [T] **accuse sb (of sth)** to say that someone has done something wrong or broken the law: *I accused her of cheating.* ◆ *He was accused of murder.*

A. Read these sentences, paying special attention to the prepositions in bold. Then say if they are true or false.

.... 1. If you say on Friday that you will finish a job **within** five days, it will be done by next Thursday.

.... 2. If you walk **along** the river, you will most probably get your feet wet.

.... 3. If the poster is **on** the wall, it is touching the wall.

.... 4. If your socks are **beneath** the bed, they are on top of the bed.

.... 5. If a classmate talks to you **concerning** your test, it means that your score was very low.

.... 6. If you throw the ball **beyond** the fence, it is between you and the fence.

.... 7. If Bryce went to the beach **despite** the weather, it was probably good weather.

.... 8. If everyone **but** Sue and Alex passed the test, only two people failed it.

.... 9. If you work **opposite** the bank, your office is across from the bank.

.... 10. If you walk **through** the park, you walk around the outer edges of it.

.... 11. If Mali fell asleep **during** the movie, he didn't see any of the movie.

.... 12. If Joe worked **throughout** March, he worked from January 1st to March 1st.

B. Underline the 15 correct prepositions. Consult the word in bold in your dictionary for helpful information.

1. Susan gave me a **rundown** (of, in, on, to) the events which led up to her car **ramming** (at, by, into, on) a shopping cart.

2. Yesterday's **lecture** (at, of, for, on) the invention of the Internet was **lacking** (at, of, in, with) specific details.

3. There was a **surge** (about, at, in, on) **demand** (of, for, in, to) baby carrots when doctors discovered that this vegetable is so **good** (at, by, for, to) people's vision.

4. Jack **quarreled** (at, for, to, with) Mary (about, by, for, in) her statement that he was **unfit** (by, for, in, to) the duties of a police officer.

5. If there is a **gap** (between, into, toward, without) the actual price and the amount I want to pay, I will **haggle** (at, for, into, with) the seller (by, for, over, to) the price.

6. At our next class, we'll **delve** (between, into, toward, without) what the primary **mode** (at, by, of, in) transportation in the country is and how it came about.

Lesson 27

Prefixes Parts of speech

A.

1. What do you think *outlast*, *outlive*, and *outrun* mean? Read this joke that uses the word *outrun* and work with a partner to figure out the meaning of *outrun*. When you think you know the meaning, retell this joke in your own words.

> One day two guys were walking through the woods when a huge bear suddenly appeared in the clearing about 100 feet in front of them. The bear saw the two men and started to head toward them. The first guy seemed to ignore the imminent danger of the situation. He hurriedly dropped his backpack, took out a pair of sneakers, and frantically began to put them on. The second guy said, "What are you doing? Sneakers won't help you outrun that bear." "Hey, I don't need to outrun the bear," the first guy replied. "I just need to outrun you."

2. The most common meaning for the prefix **out-** with verbs is "to a greater degree". See the list of Prefixes and Suffixes on pages R8–R11 of your dictionary and study the dictionary entry for the prefix **out-**.

> **out-** /aut/ *prefix* **1** (used in verbs) greater, better, further, longer, etc.: *outdo* ◆ *outnumber* **2** (used in nouns and adjectives) outside; away from: *outpatient*

B. Use the Word Bank to complete these sentences with **six** of the eight **out-** <u>verbs</u>. Remember that you may have to put the verb into the past tense to fit the sentence.

WORD BANK

outdo	outgrow	outlast	outlaw	outline	outlive	outnumber	outweigh

1. The criminals could not escape because the police .... them ten to one.
2. To succeed, a new company has to .... its competitors in overall sales.
3. At age 99, Mrs. Wilson has now .... all of her brothers and sisters.
4. Since we were short on money, the cost of the car .... every other consideration.
5. My youngest son .... his last pair of shoes in only three months.
6. His fame will definitely .... that of other rap artists.

C. Other words beginning with **out-** are linked to different meanings of the adverb **out**. Match the following <u>nouns</u> with their meanings. Use your dictionary to check your answers.

.... 1. an **outage**   a. the most important facts or ideas about something

.... 2. an **outburst**   b. a person who is no longer accepted by society

.... 3. an **outcast**   c. a criminal who lives outside society to avoid capture

.... 4. an **outlaw**   d. a period of time when electricity is cut off temporarily

.... 5. an **outline**   e. something very bad or wrong that causes you to feel great anger

.... 6. an **outrage**   f. a sudden expression of a strong feeling, especially anger

D. Out- is also used as a prefix to form <u>adjectives</u>. Fill in the missing letters of the adjective in each sentence. Each dash stands for one letter.

1. Her **outg _ _ _ _** personality made her a perfect flight attendant.
2. The capital is crowded but few people want to live in the **outl _ _ _ _** areas.
3. His answer showed his first statement to be an **outr _ _ _ _** lie.
4. The **outr _ _ _ _ _ _** cost of living in London keeps some students away.
5. When we renovated our house, we changed the **outd _ _ _ _** plumbing.

Your dictionary indicates informal vocabulary with the label *informal*. Informal vocabulary is language that is used between friends in either conversation or personal writing. It is not used in academic writing or professional speeches.

A good example is the word **ace**. The regular meaning of this word as a noun is the highest value card. However, it can be used as a verb with a related meaning, but this meaning is not formal language.

ace¹ /eɪs/ *noun* [C] **1** a playing card that has a single shape on it.

ace³ /eɪs/ *verb* [T] (*informal*) to get a very good grade on a test or exam: *She studied hard and aced all her tests.*

A. Draw lines to match up the informal adjective on the left with the neutral word on the right. Then look the words up in your dictionary and see whether you were right.

antsy	very large
bushed	relaxed
cranky	irritable
jumbo	impatient
jumpy	tired
laid-back	anxious

B. Read each statement numbered 1-10 and then match it to one of the explanations marked a-j.

.... 1. Emma's grandma is **nuts** about gardening.

.... 2. Jayden is a **couch potato**.

.... 3. Mr. Thompson frequently takes the **red-eye**.

.... 4. Isabella is a **copycat** when it comes to clothing.

.... 5. Jacob is working at a computer company, but he is still pretty **green**.

.... 6. Benjamin accidentally **spilled the beans** about the surprise party.

.... 7. When it comes to hospitals, Sophia is **chicken**.

.... 8. Michael is in a **jam** again.

.... 9. Kevin likes to **pig out** late at night.

.... 10. Everyone agrees that little Abigail is quite a **handful**.

a. This person does what his or her friends do.

b. This person has a very strong interest in an activity.

c. This person is difficult to control.

d. This person is afraid.

e. This person watches a lot of television.

f. This person has very little experience.

g. This person flies at night.

h. This person eats too much.

i. This person cannot keep a secret.

j. This person is in a difficult situation.

C. Using informal vocabulary can help you sound more friendly, so it is important for you to learn about this kind of language. Scan your dictionary for **three** examples of informal words or expressions and write them here along with the meaning in your own words.

1. .... = ...

2. .... = ...

3. .... = ...

Idioms with body parts Informal language

English contains many idioms using parts of the human body. How many of these idioms do you know already? Working for two minutes either on your own or with a partner, write as many idioms as you can think of with any body part such as **hand**, **ear**, **mouth**, **leg**, etc. You can check them in your dictionary.

To find the meaning of an idiom in your dictionary, look up the first important word in the idiom (for example, **change**). The idioms containing the word **change** are listed in the section marked **IDM**.

If the meaning is given at a different place in the dictionary, there is an arrow that sends you to the right place.

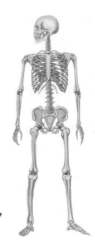

hand¹ 🔊 /hænd/ *noun*
> PART OF BODY **1** [C] the part of your body at the end of your arm, including your fingers and thumb

IDM **at hand 1** near in space or time: *Help is close at hand.* **2** being dealt with at this time: *We need to focus on the task at hand.*
be an old hand (at sth) ⊃ **old**
by hand 1 done by a person and not by machine: *I had to do all the sewing by hand.* **2** not by mail: *The letter was delivered by hand.*
change hands ⊃ **change¹**

change¹ 🔊 /tʃeɪndʒ/ *verb*
> BECOME/MAKE DIFFERENT **1** [I, T] to become different or to make someone or something different

IDM **change hands** to pass from one owner to another

A. Draw lines to match up the verb with the body part and the correct meaning.

VERB	BODY PART	MEANING
change	hairs	to make fun of someone by trying to make him/her believe something that is not true
split	sb's leg	to try hard to think of something or remember something
pull	face	to pass from one owner to another
rack	an arm and a leg	to cost a large amount of money
cost	hands	to lose the respect of other people
lose	your brains	to pay too much attention in an argument to differences that are very small and not important

B. Use the Word Bank to complete the idioms in these sentences with parts of the body. (If you need more help, look up the entry for the word in **bold** in each sentence.)

WORD BANK

> neck ear tongue hand head wrist skin fingers

1. I grew up in this neighborhood, so I **know** it like the back of my ....

2. We're not sure what we'll do in Madrid. We're going to **play** it by ....

3. Off the **top** of your ...., how many people do you think were in the meeting?

4. Oh, what's his name? It's on the **tip** of my ....

5. Some of the customers can be a real **pain** in the ....

6. The criminal just got a **slap** on the .... instead of a more serious punishment.

7. A good boss has to have **thick** .... in that kind of job.

8. I will **cross** my .... that you get that job in New York.

C. What do you think these idioms mean? Choose the best meaning for each one and then check your dictionary to see how well you did.

....*e*.... 1. have egg on your face

.... 2. out of hand

.... 3. behind sb's back

.... 4. give sb the cold shoulder

.... 5. keep an eye on sb/sth

.... 6. put your foot in your mouth

.... 7. neck and neck

a. not under control

b. without someone's knowledge or agreement

c. equal or level

d. to say or do something that upsets or embarrasses someone

e. to be made to look stupid

f. to take care of someone or something

g. to treat someone in an unfriendly way

Idioms with numbers Informal language

English contains many idioms using numbers such as **one** and **two** or sequence words such as **first** and **last**.

once[1] /wʌns/ *adv.* **1** one time only; on one occasion: *I've only been to Mexico once.*

IDM all at once **1** suddenly: *All at once she got up and left the room.* **2** all together; at the same time: *People began talking all at once.*
once in a blue moon (*informal*) very rarely; almost never: *We live in Amarillo, so I only go to Dallas once in a blue moon.*

A. Use the Word Bank to complete the idioms in these sentences. Look up the underlined words to find the idioms in your dictionary.

WORD BANK

| in two | on the dot | in her sixties | kill two birds with one stone |
| at long last | all at once | in the first place | once upon a time |

1. My father said, "No, you cannot drive to Los Angeles with Matt. _____, you've got work to do, and on top of that, he's not a good driver, so it's not safe."

2. Jeanine and I were walking in the park when _____ the sky opened and torrential rain began to fall.

3. _____, I made 100 on a test in Mrs. Greer's class. I've been trying for ages, but her tests are incredibly tough.

4. Mrs. Wilson is extremely punctual, and her class starts every day at 9 o'clock _____.

5. I'm starving, so if you'll cut that sandwich _____, I'll take half.

6. My aunt Sue must be _____ because she's a little older than my dad, and he's 58.

7. If I go to the mall, I can _____. I can buy a shirt and then visit my friend who's working at a jewelry store there.

8. _____, a young girl lived in a small house in a magical forest.

B. Answer the following questions about these idioms.

1. If a bus company has a sign that says "**First come, first served**," do they accept reservations?
   _____

2. Are you **on a first-name basis** with your teacher? With your parents? With your boss? _____

3. If you are allergic to nuts and aren't crazy about cheese and someone offers you a chunk of cheddar or some pistachios, which is **the lesser of two evils** here? _____

4. If you think someone is **one of a kind**, do you have a positive or negative image of the person? _____

5. If Jorge is **having second thoughts** about his decision to move to Miami, what does this mean?
   _____

6. If Mrs. Meed said she **put all her eggs in one basket**, is she talking about cooking? _____

7. If the teacher tells her class that her lesson seems to **go in one ear and out the other**, is she happy about the lesson? _____

8. What is the **third-to-last** month of the year? _____

9. If José **had the last word**, was he probably shopping, sleeping, or speaking? _____

10. If Connor and Olivia bought a gift for **one another**, how many gifts did they buy? _____

11. If Keith plays tennis **once in a while**, does he play every other day? _____

12. If your teacher allows you to rewrite your paper **just this once**, is this a usual event? _____

C. Check the many idioms with **once** or **one** in your dictionary. Write **three** new idioms and their meanings or an example here to help you remember each.

Idiom 1. _____ = _____

Idiom 2. _____ = _____

Idiom 3. _____ = _____

Phrasal verbs are two- and three-word phrases that are composed of verbs plus prepositions and/or adverbs. Like an idiom, the meaning of a phrasal verb is different than the meaning of the words that make it up. In your dictionary, phrasal verbs are in a separate section of the entry, and are marked with the label **PHRV**.

> **call sth off** to cancel something: *The baseball game was called off because of rain.*

> **get along with sb** to have a friendly relationship with someone: *Do you get along well with your co-workers?* ◆ *We're not close friends, but we get along pretty well with each other.*

A. Match the beginning of each sentence with the best ending. Study the phrasal verbs in **bold** carefully.

.... 1. I **turned down**	a. late because of the bad weather.
.... 2. The boys **turned up**	b. the exam until the following week.
.... 3. He **put away**	c. , so we went outside to play.
.... 4. He **put off**	d. an excuse for arriving so late.
.... 5. We **shopped around**	e. people who speak six different languages.
.... 6. The bank has **set up**	f. for the best price for a new car.
.... 7. Our class is **made up of**	g. once again.
.... 8. Breanna **made up**	h. his request to borrow $100 from me.
.... 9. Marcus **let** us **down**	i. a new branch in Denver.
.... 10. The rain finally **let up**	j. the tools when the job was done.

B. The following sentences all contain phrasal verbs. In each case, choose the correct adverb/preposition or verb from the options given in parentheses.

1. Our flight **took** (*off*, *out*, *up*) on time, but we arrived late just the same.
2. Aidan and Noah had an argument, but now they have **made** (*back*, *off*, *up*).
3. When I (*found*, *got*, *took*) **back** from vacation, there were several messages waiting for me.
4. I (*looked*, *made*, *saw*) **through** the classified ads to see if I could find an apartment to rent.
5. My father used to love music. He **took** (*after*, *away*, *over*) his father.
6. Evy **picked** (*back*, *out*, *up*) her friends from the airport and took them to their hotel.
7. The crossword puzzle was really hard, and Ethan eventually (*gave*, *made*, *threw*) **up**.
8. It was so hot that two people **passed** (*off*, *out*, *up*).
9. The police are upset that the criminal **got** (*in*, *off*, *up*).
10. When Chloe was cleaning her room, she (*came*, *found*, *made*) **across** her first driver's license.
11. Mia couldn't hear the radio well, so she **turned** (*away*, *over*, *up*) the volume.
12. At my first job, I didn't earn much, but I (*got*, *made*, *put*) **by**.

C. Scan your dictionary for **five** new phrasal verbs. Write the phrasal verbs and a meaning or example that can help you remember the word. Share your new vocabulary with your classmates.

Phrasal Verb 1. .... = ...
Phrasal Verb 2. .... = ...
Phrasal Verb 3. .... = ...
Phrasal Verb 4. .... = ...
Phrasal Verb 5. .... = ...

Topic collocations Collocations

Simply put, a collocation is a combination of words that is common. We say *write an e-mail* (NOT ~~make an e-mail~~), *long eyelashes* (NOT ~~big eyelashes~~), and *get experience* (NOT ~~take experience~~).

Knowing collocations will make your English better. Your speaking and writing will sound more natural. In addition, your reading and listening will improve because you can comprehend the whole phrase instead of trying to understand word by word.

Your **Oxford American Dictionary** has Topic Collocations boxes with many useful examples of common combinations, related to a range of different topics.

col·lo·ca·tion /ˌkɑləˈkeɪʃn/ *noun* [C] (**ENG. LANG. ARTS**) a combination of words in a language, which happens very often and more frequently than would happen by chance: *"Resounding success"* and *"crying shame"* are English collocations.

TOPIC COLLOCATIONS

E-mail and the Internet
e-mail
- **have/set up** an e-mail account
- **receive/get/open** an e-mail
- **write/send/answer/reply to/forward/delete** an e-mail
- **check/read/access** your e-mail
- **open/send/contain** an attachment
- **attach** a file/picture/document

A. Underline the **two** collocations that are possible in each of these sentences. For help, study the Topic Collocations box for the word(s) shown at the end of each sentence.

1. **Diet and exercise** I try to (**go to, take off, work out at**) the gym every day.
2. **Diet and exercise** I think I have (**gained, made up, put on**) a few pounds.
3. **Driving** Do you know what to do if you (**have, get, take**) a flat tire?
4. **Driving** Can you drive (**a gas pedal, a manual, a stick shift**)?
5. **Jobs** Do you think she will (**find, get, let**) a job at the bank?
6. **Jobs** Did you (**exit, resign from, quit**) your job?
7. **Money** He can't afford (**to buy, to handle, to pay for**) a new car.
8. **Money** We live on (**a cash machine, $3,000 a month, a pension**).
9. **Restaurants** You can pay (**at the counter, at the register, at the menu**).
10. **Restaurants** Let's (**cut, divide up, split**) the bill, OK?
11. **Shopping** Do you prefer to pay (**in cash, with money, by card**)?
12. **Shopping** Did she (**ask for, get, take**) a refund?
13. **Television and movies** Please (**change, replace, switch**) the channel.
14. **Television and movies** If you want, I can (**burn, copy, let**) a DVD for you.
15. **Travel and tourism** You must (**check, collect, deliver**) your luggage immediately!
16. **Travel and tourism** Did you (**make, pack, unpack**) your suitcase?
17. **The weather** When the rain (**lets up, stops, turns off**), I'll go outside again.
18. **The weather** They are (**forecasting, foretelling, predicting**) 14 inches of snow for tomorrow!

B. Complete the following collocations with a word from the Topic Collocations box. More than one answer may be possible. Use only words from your dictionary.

1. **Phones** .... a phone call .... a text
2. **Clothes and appearance** .... a haircut be .... as a pirate
3. **Music** be into .... an album
4. **Illnesses and injuries** catch .... your ankle
5. **Animals** insects .... hatches

The parrot joke Collocations

par·rot /ˈpærət/ *noun* [C] a type of tropical bird with a curved beak and usually with very bright feathers. **Parrots** that are kept as pets often copy what people say.

foul¹ /faʊl/ *adj.* **1** that smells or tastes disgusting: *This coffee tastes foul!* ♦ *foul city air* **2** very bad or unpleasant: *Careful what you say – he's got a foul temper* (= he becomes angry very easily). ♦ *foul weather* **3** (used about language) very rude; full of swearing: *foul language*

Read this joke and then answer the questions about the information. Circle any words that you do not know and look them up in your dictionary.

One day, a rather lonely man went into a pet shop to purchase a talking parrot. At first, everything was going great, but the parrot ended up causing trouble because it constantly used so much foul language. Buying a parrot had seemed like such a good idea in the
5 beginning, but now the owner was really annoyed by the bird's nasty habit. When the man finally couldn't take the parrot's inappropriate language any more, he yelled at the bird, "Shut up!" but this just made the bird mad, and it started swearing more than ever. At that point, the owner was so mad that he threw the bird into the freezer.
10 For the very first few seconds the bird kicked and put up a struggle. Then it suddenly gave up and got very quiet.

In fact, after a couple of minutes of silence, the owner was so worried about the parrot that he opened up the freezer door to see if the parrot was all right. The bird calmly climbed onto the man's
15 outstretched arm and said, "I am truly sorry about the trouble I gave you. I really appreciate everything that you have done for me. I'll do my best to improve my vocabulary from now on."

The man was astounded. He couldn't understand the amazing transformation that had come over the parrot, but the bird's
20 peaceful manner was a welcome change from its previous nasty behavior. Then the parrot asked in a very shaky voice, "By the way, do you mind if I ask this question: what did that chicken do?"

A. Put these six statements in the correct order. Write the correct number in front of the sentence.

.... a. The man released the parrot.

.... b. The man put the parrot in the freezer.

.... c. The parrot no longer used foul language.

.... d. The parrot saw the chicken.

.... e. The man bought a pet.

.... f. The man was upset by the parrot's swearing.

B. Which word or phrase means…?

.... 1. very surprised (line 18)

.... 2. to shout (line 7)

.... 3. in a way that is not worried or angry (line 14)

.... 4. very rude; full of swearing (line 3)

.... 5. starting at the present time and continuing forever (line 17)

C. Use the Word Bank to complete these important word combinations from the joke.

WORD BANK

arm struggle peaceful mad couple now
shaky amazing way foul cause mind

1. .... language

2. a .... of things

3. a .... voice

4. put up a ....

5. .... trouble

6. from .... on

7. make somebody ....

8. do you .... if…

9. his outstretched ....

10. an .... transformation

11. a .... manner

12. by the ....

Prepositions after AWL vocabulary Collocations

Some words are followed by specific prepositions, and it is important for you to use the correct preposition after these words. The twenty-two words practiced in this lesson are from the Academic Word List. Your dictionary can help you select the correct preposition.

> **ex·pert**[1] 🔊 **AWL** /ˈɛkspərt/ *noun* [C] **an expert (at/ in/on sth)** a person who has a lot of special knowledge or skill: *He's an expert on the history of rock music.* ◆ *She's a computer expert.* ◆ *Let me try – I'm an expert at parking cars in small spaces.*

A. Use the Word Bank to complete the prepositions in these sentences. You will need to use some of them twice. Then read the statements and write TRUE or FALSE in the Answer column. If you need more help, look up the entry for the word in **bold** in each sentence. The first sentence has been done for you.

WORD BANK   against   as   for   in   into   of   on   to   with

	Which preposition?	Meaning: true or false?	Answer
1.	Jason is an **expert** _on_ college football results.	He knows a lot about this subject.	true
2.	Sports are not so **relevant** .... my life.	Sports are very important to me.	
3.	There was no **evidence** .... a crime.	A crime certainly happened.	
4.	The risk of failure is **inherent** .... every business.	All businesses may fail.	
5.	Brittany is **aware** .... the problem.	She knows about the problem.	
6.	The results of today's test are **consistent** .... those of previous studies.	The results are different.	
7.	**Exposure** .... rain caused the bike to rust.	The rain improved the bike.	
8.	My boss has a **bias** .... younger workers.	Younger workers dislike my boss.	
9.	The other students unfairly **labeled** her .... stupid.	They wrote unfair things about her.	
10.	It was a great experience for me to **interact** .... the kids!	I spent time talking with the kids.	
11.	The movie gave me an **insight** .... the perils of war.	The special effects were amazing.	
12.	The humor in the story **compensated** .... the poor plot.	I liked some things about the story.	

B. Use the Word Bank to complete the following questions. Then decide which is the better answer for the question. If you need more help, look up the entry for the word in **bold** in each sentence.

WORD BANK   for   from   in   of   on   to   with

1. What was the most important **factor** .... his choice of a career?   a. engineering   b. salary
2. Which color is more **similar** .... pink?   a. red   b. green
3. What might be the **source** .... a leak?   a. a broken chin   b. a broken pipe
4. Which is **derived** .... milk?   a. calcium   b. cheese
5. Which word has the main **stress** .... the first syllable?   a. devote   b. shadow
6. Which date is **prior** .... the publication of this book?   a. May 1, 1922   b. May 1, 2022
7. Who **prohibited** the students .... watching that movie?   a. the students   b. their parents
8. Which sport has a higher **incidence** .... injuries?   a. golf   b. soccer
9. Which of these **supplement** their diet .... insects?   a. birds   b. bees
10. What's the best **technique** .... staying in shape?   a. watch a DVD   b. do exercise

Academic Word List collocations Collocations

Knowing the Academic Word List is important, but to use the words correctly, you need to know their most common collocations. Your **Oxford American Dictionary** has AWL Collocations boxes with many useful examples of how to use items from several of the AWL word families.

> **AWL COLLOCATIONS**
>
> **emphasis**
> **emphasis** *noun*
> special importance or attention
> considerable, great, strong | particular, special | renewed | increased
> *There is a strong emphasis on math and science at the school.* ♦ *She focuses on Russian literature, with particular emphasis on the works of Dostoevsky.*
> place, put, lay
> *The new information-based economy placed greater emphasis on new technical knowledge.*

> **emphasize** *verb*
> strongly, rightly | consistently | continually, repeatedly
> *The guidelines strongly emphasize the importance of physical activity in health promotion.* ♦ *He consistently emphasizes this theme throughout his work.*

A. Cross out the **one** collocation that is NOT possible in each of the following sentences. For help, study the AWL Collocations boxes at the entry shown at the end of each sentence.

1. Unfortunately, the new, more fuel-efficient cars are not (**broadly**, **readily**, **widely**) **available** to consumers yet.   **available**

2. How did you (**arrive at**, **come to**, **reach**, **train**) that **conclusion**?   **conclude**

3. Without a doubt, the participants' education level was a **contributing** (**fact**, **factor**) in the experiment's result.   **contribute**

4. Under our new boss, the atmosphere at work now (**depletes**, **fosters**, **stifles**) **creativity**.   **create**

5. I got a B+ on my report because of the (**particular**, **special**, **wide**) **emphasis** I put on Lincoln's early life.   **emphasis**

6. I need to get (an **accurate**, a **rough**, a **sufficient**) **estimate** of what my first year of college will cost.   **estimate**

7. After (a **careful**, an **increasing**, a **rigorous**, a **thorough**) **evaluation** of my checkup results, the doctor advised me to give up coffee.   **evaluate**

8. The teacher told us to explain our position on the issue and then (**present**, **propel**, **provide**) **evidence** to support our position.   **evident**

9. Doctors depend on software that can help them make (**accurate**, **correct**, **hollow**) **identification** of the beginning of cancer.   **identify**

10. The author's use of so many descriptive adjectives is a (**daunting**, **striking**, **vivid**) **illustration** of the depth of her writing ability.   **illustrate**

11. The insurance company will (**conduct**, **persuade**, **undertake**) an **investigation** of both drivers' claims.   **investigate**

12. Even with modern technology, meteorologists cannot (**accurately**, **gratefully**, **reliably**) **predict** the weather for a region.   **predict**

13. Our professor will **rely** (**carefull**y, **exclusively**, **solely**) on our top three exam grades to calculate our overall course grade.   **rely**

14. To me, that researcher's **theoretical** (**approach**, **framework**, **routine**) is rather far-fetched.   **theory**

B. Study the AWL Collocations boxes in your dictionary. Write **five** collocations that are new to you. Write the AWL word family where the box is located in parentheses and a brief explanation of the phrase.

Collocation 1. .... (at ....) = ...

Collocation 2. .... (at ....) = ...

Collocation 3. .... (at ....) = ...

Collocation 4. .... (at ....) = ...

Collocation 5. .... (at ....) = ...

A difficult choice Collocations

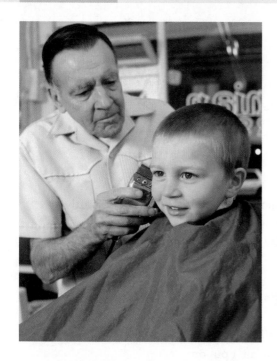

A young boy entered a barbershop, and the barber whispered to his customer, "This is the stupidest kid in the world. I'm going to prove it to you."

The barber placed a dollar bill in one hand and two quarters in
5 the other and asked the young boy, "Which do you want, son?" The boy said, "That's easy," took the quarters, and walked out of the barbershop richer than he had been just a few minutes before. The customer was somewhat surprised.

"What did I tell you?" said the barber. "That kid always does the
10 same thing!"

Later, when the customer left the shop, he saw the same young boy coming out of the nearby ice-cream store. "Hey, son! May I ask you a question? Why did you take the quarters instead of the dollar bill? You are old enough to know better."

15 The boy took a bite of his ice-cream cone and said with a slight grin, "Because the day I take the dollar, the game is over!"

A. Which word from the text means … ?

1. .... to speak very quietly to someone so that other people cannot what you are saying (line 1)

2. .... to put something in a particular position (line 4)

3. .... very small; not important or serious (line 15)

4. .... a little (line 8)

5. .... to use facts or evidence to show that something is true (line 3)

6. .... a person who buys goods or services (line 2)

7. .... not far away in distance (line 12)

8. .... finished (line 16)

> **cone** /koʊn/ *noun* [C] **1** a solid shape that has a round base and gets narrower, making a point at the top **2** an object of this shape: *an ice-cream cone ◆ orange traffic cones along the side of the road* **3** the hard dry fruit of a some types of tree: *a pine cone*

B. Use the Word Bank to complete these important combinations based on the joke.

WORD BANK
| ask before bill cone enough game same |
| slight somewhat store take world |

1. a dollar ....
2. the stupidest kid in the ....
3. a few minutes ....
4. .... surprised
5. always do the .... thing
6. an ice-cream .... OR ....
7. .... a question
8. old .... to know better
9. .... a bite of something
10. a .... grin
11. the .... is over

C Do you find this joke funny? Write a short paragraph in which you explain what is funny about it. In your writing, use as many of the new vocabulary words and phrases as possible.

....
....
....
....
....
....

Mathematics uses many special vocabulary items such as **calculator**, **geometry**, and **right angle**. These words are marked in your **Oxford American Dictionary** with the label MATH. In this lesson, you will practice vocabulary that is related to mathematics.

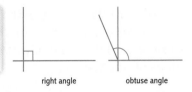

an·gle¹ 🔊 /'æŋgl/ *noun* [C] **1** (**MATH**) the space between two lines or surfaces that meet, measured in degrees: *a right angle* (= an angle of 90°) ◆ *at an angle of 40°* ◆ *The three angles of a triangle add up to 180°.*

right angle   obtuse angle

A. Match the vocabulary item to the mathematics example. The dictionary entry for the words **equal**, **decimal**, **multiple**, etc. will help you.

_j_   1. **equals sign**

.... 2. **decimals**

.... 3. **multiples of 4**

.... 4. **negative integers**

.... 5. **even numbers**

.... 6. **odd numbers**

.... 7. **percentage**

.... 8. **denominator**

.... 9. **fractions**

.... 10. **equation**

.... 11. **numerator**

.... 12. **ordinal numbers**

a. $x^2 + 2x = 15$

b. -10, -6, -3, -1

c. 50%

d. ²⁄₃, ½, ³⁄₅, ⁹⁄₁₀

e. 0.2, 0.75, 0.001, 0.86

f. 8, 16, 12, 20

g. 2, 22, 30, 88

h. 3, 19, 41, 75

i. 1st, 2nd, 3rd, 4th

j. =

k. the number 2 in ²⁄₃

l. the number 3 in ²⁄₃

B. Answer these mathematics questions. If you need help, look up the **bold** words in your dictionary.

1. How many degrees are there in a **right angle**?

2. Calculate the **area** of a **square** that is 7 inches long.

3. How many sides of an **isosceles triangle** are the same length?

4. What is the **common denominator** in ½ + ⅓ = ⅚?

5. 11, 12, 13, 14, 15 – Which two of these are **prime numbers**?

6. Can two **parallel** lines ever be **perpendicular** to each other?

7. How do you write three **cubed**? Calculate the value of three **cubed**.

8. What is the **square root** of sixteen?

9. What is the **average** of 5, 12, and 7?

10. To find the **sum**, do you **add**, **subtract**, **multiply**, or **divide**?

Science vocabulary Content areas

Science uses many special vocabulary terms such as **hypothesis**, **calcium**, **molar**, and **gravity**. These words are marked in your **Oxford American Dictionary** with the labels GENERAL SCIENCE, BIOLOGY, CHEMISTRY, or PHYSICS. In this lesson, you will practice vocabulary related to these areas of science.

mo·lar /'moʊlər/ *noun* [C] (BIOLOGY) one of the large teeth in the back of your mouth ⊃ Look at **canine**, **incisor**.

A. Put each word in its correct category.

copper	nickel	circuit breaker	pancreas	uranium
test tube	laser	primate	liver	butterfly
larva	amphibian	microscope	tungsten	parasite
appendix	lung	beaker	lithium	Achilles tendon
kidney	mollusk	mercury	thermometer	

a creature	an instrument	a metal	a body part
1.	1.	1.	1.
2.	2.	2.	2.
3.	3.	3.	3.
4.	4.	4.	4.
5.	5.	5.	5.
6.	6.	6.	6.

B. Answer these science questions. If you need help, look up the **bold** words in your dictionary. Circle the correct answer in each sentence.

1. A (**fingerprint**, **flame**, **scale**) can be used to measure something's weight.
2. A (**fin**, **petal**, **school**) of fish is a large group of fish.
3. A green plant has (**chlorophyll**, **fangs**, **pincers**).
4. If you (**distill**, **ferment**, **immunize**) water, the result is pure water.
5. There are (**firecrackers**, **incisors**, **tentacles**) in our mouths.
6. (**Foam**, **Glucose**, **Sediment**) might settle at the bottom of a river.
7. The informal word for this part of the body is your belly button: (**collarbone**, **thorax**, **navel**).
8. (**Cornea**, **Fiber**, **Saliva**) is the liquid in our mouths.
9. A herbivore might eat a (**butterfly**, **fern**, **mammal**).
10. A diagram that shows the steps in a process is called a (**flow chart**, **periodic table**, **statistic**).
11. Most fish have (**clones**, **fumes**, **gills**).
12. Flowers have (**clavicles**, **plankton**, **pollen**).
13. The process a living being goes through as it grows from one stage of life to the next is called its (**life cycle**, **life expectancy**, **life span**).
14. After two animals **breed**, they may have (**clots**, **offspring**, **spines**).

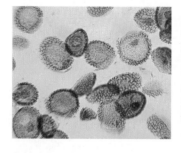

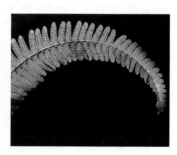

Social studies is a useful course because it prepares people to be knowledgeable citizens of their countries and the world. Social studies vocabulary is marked in your **Oxford American Dictionary** with the labels GEOGRAPHY, POLITICS, or HISTORY. In this lesson, you will practice key vocabulary related to social studies.

> **'social studies** *noun* [pl.] a subject taught in schools that studies human society and that includes history, geography, government, etc.

A. Write L or W to indicate whether these key geography terms refer to areas of **land** or **water**.

	1. **bayou**		6. **stream**		11. **prairie**		16. **lake**
	2. **strait**		7. **pond**		12. **plateau**		17. **spring**
	3. **plain**		8. **jungle**		13. **meadow**		18. **peak**
	4. **canal**		9. **lagoon**		14. **isthmus**		19. **marsh**
	5. **desert**		10. **flood**		15. **ocean**		20. **gulf**

B. Answer these questions about politics. If you need help, look up the **bold** words in your dictionary.

1. What do people in several U.S. states do on **Super Tuesday**? ....

2. Which of these do you sing – **the Stars and Stripes** or **the Star-Spangled Banner**? ....

3. **Uncle Sam** is portrayed as an old man, but who are we really talking about when we mention his name? ....

4. What is the **Secretary of State** responsible for? ....

5. What does **NASA** stand for? ....

C. Fill in each of the blanks with one of the political terms from the Word Bank.

> WORD BANK
>
> ballot   ratify   veto   green card   national anthem
> precinct   treaty   alien   polling place   first lady

1. At election time, citizens mark a .... at a .... in the .... where they live.

2. The President of the U.S. can negotiate a .... with another country, but Congress has to .... it before it takes effect.

3. To live and work in the U.S., every .... must apply for a ....

4. At the opening ceremony, the President and the .... stood during the singing of the ....

5. If the president is not in favor of a bill, he can .... it.

D. How well do you know history vocabulary? Write A by the **two** places, B by the **five** people, and C by the **five** events or periods.

	1. **dictator**		5. **ground zero**		9. **knight**
	2. **the Holocaust**		6. **the Revolutionary War**		10. **ancestor**
	3. **Prohibition**		7. **Founding Father**		11. **the Reformation**
	4. **Dixie**		8. **Pilgrim**		12. **medieval**

Sports vocabulary Content areas

Sports uses many special vocabulary terms. Some terms such as **team** and **rematch** are used in many different sports, while others are used in one or two sports only, such as **ace** (tennis), **goalkeeper** (soccer), and **putt** (golf). These words are marked in your **Oxford American Dictionary** with the label SPORTS. In this lesson, you will practice vocabulary that is related to sports.

goal·keep·er /ˈɡoʊlˌkipər/ (also informal **goal·ie** /ˈɡoʊli/) noun [C] (**SPORTS**) a player whose job is to stop the ball from going into his or her own team's goal in a game of SOCCER: *The goalkeeper made a terrific save.* ⊃ See picture at **soccer**.

re·match /ˈrimætʃ/ noun [C, usually sing.] (**SPORTS**) a match or game played again between the same people or teams, especially because neither side won the first match or game

A. Put these 30 sports terms with their correct sport.

doubleheader	marathon	volley	quarterback	serve
shoot	match	lap	strike (sb) out	backboard
sprint	dribble	touchdown	tee	batter
love	catcher	backhand	tackle	home run
end zone	running back	green	club	shortstop
slam-dunk	racket	course	outfield	scrimmage

football	basketball	running	tennis	golf	baseball
1.	1.	1.	1.	1.	1.
2.	2.	2.	2.	2.	2.
3.	3.	3.	3.	3.	3.
4.	4.		4.	4.	4.
5.			5.		5.
6.			6.		6.
					7.

B. Write **course**, **court**, or **field** to indicate where these sports are played.

1. a football ....
2. a tennis ....
3. a basketball ....
4. a golf ....
5. a baseball ....
6. a soccer ....

C. Answer these sports questions. If you need help, look up the **bold** words in your dictionary.

1. If you are in the **penalty box**, is this a good or a bad thing? ....
2. Who would you find on the **mound** – the catcher or the pitcher? ....
3. If a race ends in a **photo finish**, how close is the winner to the runner-up? ....
4. Is the **baton** that one athlete passes to another a piece of paper, a ball, or a stick? ....
5. If Team A's game with Team B ends in a **draw**, who was the winner? ....
6. Where do people practice **spelunking**? ....
7. Which of these is related to baseball – **Little League**, **NBA**, **Super Bowl**? ....
8. In what sport could a participant make a **pit stop**? ....
9. Which of these events requires athletes to do the most sports – **a marathon**, **a decathlon**, **a pentathlon**? ....
10. If a team has just won their **quarterfinal** game, how many more games do they have to play to win the **championship**? ....

Frequent nouns Oxford 3000 words

All the words in this lesson are nouns from the **Oxford 3000** list of important words selected by experts in English teaching. These 3,000 words are shown in the main section of the dictionary in a different color from the other words and with a key symbol 🔑 immediately following.

blade 🔑 /bleɪd/ *noun* [C] **1** the flat, sharp part of a knife, a pair of scissors, etc. ⊃ See picture at **kitchen**. **2** one of the flat, wide parts that spin around on a plane, etc.: *a propeller blade* **3** a long, thin leaf of grass: *a blade of grass*

blood 🔑 /blʌd/ *noun* [U] **1** (**HEALTH**) the red liquid that flows through the body: *Blood was pouring from a cut on his knee.* ♦ *The heart pumps blood around the body.* ♦ *He lost a lot of blood in the accident.*

A. Answer the following questions about these 60 nouns.

1. Which two CANNOT be red?
   blood cheek decoration dot fence heel onion pace stone towel wheel wage

2. Which two CANNOT usually be found in the kitchen?
   cabinet drawer faucet fee flour grade jam jelly oven sauce stove wire

3. Which two are NOT usually hard?
   blade brick branch hammer chain pocket ruler shelf scissors screw sleeve weapon

4. Which two are NOT usually negative?
   anxiety argument award colleague criminal funeral injury murder opponent poison refusal warning

5. Which two are NOT living?
   attorney bear bowl boyfriend bush citizen customer executive mouse root steam visitor

B. Put these 28 words in their correct categories.

WORD BANK

ankle border consumer desert elbow fashion fur glove heel hill jacket leather nephew ocean partner passenger region sailor scientist shoulder silk skin slope soldier underwear valley waist wrist

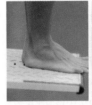 

body parts	things you wear	person	geography
1.	8.	15.	22.
2.	9.	16.	23.
3.	10.	17.	24.
4.	11.	18.	25.
5.	12.	19.	26.
6.	13.	20.	27.
7.	14.	21.	28.

C. New words

Write down any new words that you have learned in this lesson and then look up their definitions.

Word 1. .... = ...

Word 2. .... = ...

Word 3. .... = ...

Word 4. .... = ...

Word 5. .... = ...

Frequent verbs Oxford 3000 words

All the words in this lesson are verbs from the **Oxford 3000** list of important words selected by experts in English teaching. These 3,000 words are shown in the main section of the dictionary in a different color from the other words and with a key symbol 🔑 immediately following.

guard[2] 🔑 /gɑrd/ *verb* [T] **1** to keep someone or something safe from other people: *The building was guarded by men with dogs.* ♦ *agents guarding the president* **SYN protect 2** to watch over someone and prevent him/her from escaping: *The prisoner was closely guarded on the way to the courthouse.*

guide[2] 🔑 /gaɪd/ *verb* [T] **1** to help a person or a group of people to find the right way or direction to go: *He guided us through the busy streets to our hotel.* **2** to have an influence on someone or something: *I was guided by your advice.*

A. Answer the following questions about these 64 verbs.

1. Which two of these usually have a negative connotation (meaning)?
   admire   blame   clap   delight   earn   encourage   gain   guarantee   impress   praise   shock   smile

2. Which two of these usually have a positive connotation?
   argue   bother   explode   frighten   harm   protest   reform   regret   reject   rescue   sink   yawn

3. Which two of these add –ed to form the past tense?
   blow   breed   burst   cast   catch   crush   forgive   hit   hurt   ruin   shoot   spread

4. Which two of these are usually done by a thing or an animal, not a person?
   argue   burst   cheat   clap   complain   deny   praise   regret   sting   swear   sweat   yawn

5. Which two of these usually involve saying something?
   apologize   become   complain   delay   dig   drive   hang   invest   kick   lose   ruin   shoot   smash   steal   tear   unite

B. Where might you hear these verb examples? Match the phrase with its most likely location.

A. **doctor's office**   B. **police station**   C. **classroom**   D. **radio station**

.... 1. "**Calculate** the area of triangle ABC."

.... 2. "We **arrested** two people last week."

.... 3. "If your ankle begins to **swell**, **rub** this on it."

.... 4. "We **broadcast** in the southern area only."

.... 5. "When is it difficult for you to **breathe**?"

.... 6. "We **captured** the young man who was fleeing the scene."

.... 7. "Can you please **cough** for me**?**"

.... 8. "You are in tenth grade now, so you should know how to **behave** properly."

.... 9. "We didn't **forecast** today's rain, but let's hear now what the outlook is for tomorrow."

.... 10. "We will spare no effort to **hunt** down the killers."

C. New words

Write down any new words that you have learned in this lesson and then look up their definitions.

Word 1. .... = ...

Word 2. .... = ...

Word 3. .... = ...

Word 4. .... = ...

Word 5. .... = ...

Frequent adjectives Oxford 3000 words

All the words in this lesson are adjectives from the **Oxford 3000** list of important words selected by experts in English teaching. These 3,000 words are shown in the main section of the dictionary in a different color from the other words and with a key symbol 🔑 immediately following.

> **an·nu·al** 🔑 AWL /ˈænyuəl/ adj. **1** happening or done once a year or every year: *the company's annual report* ◆ *an annual event* **2** relating to a period of one year: *Her annual income is $30,000.*

> **out·stand·ing** 🔑 /ˌaʊtˈstændɪŋ/ adj. **1** very good; excellent: *Your work in this course has been outstanding.* **2** not yet paid or done: *outstanding debts*

A. Answer the following questions about these 36 adjectives.

1. Which three adjectives are NOT usually used to describe people?
   annual   ashamed   blond   concerned   confident   grateful   impressed   parallel   patient   scared   steep   willing

2. Which three adjectives might normally be used to describe a cake?
   ancient   approximate   blank   brief   bored   deaf   damp   glad   light   rich   steep   sweet

3. Which three adjectives might be used to describe music?
   contemporary   covered   loud   loyal   narrow   nuclear   occupied   pointed   pregnant   shaped   shiny   soft

B. In each group of four adjectives, circle the one that has a negative connotation (meaning).

1. **accurate   cruel   prompt   remarkable**
2. **awful   faithful   genuine   innocent**
3. **brilliant   generous   grave   outstanding**
4. **bitter   fancy   pure   sincere**
5. **amusing   dull   ideal   loyal**
6. **contemporary   honest   lacking   precise**
7. **awkward   beautiful   clever   fresh**
8. **brilliant   famous   gentle   immoral**

C. Add the correct adjective ending: -able, -al, -ern, -ful, -ive or -ly.

1. **profession**..........
2. **reason**..........
3. **region**..........
4. **week**..........
5. **suit**..........
6. **origin**..........
7. **west**..........
8. **mass**..........
9. **cheer**..........
10. **enjoy**..........
11. **physic**..........
12. **comfort**..........
13. **live**..........
14. **north**..........
15. **faith**..........

D. New words

Write down any new words that you have learned in this lesson and then look up their definitions.

Word 1. .... = ...
Word 2. .... = ...
Word 3. .... = ...
Word 4. .... = ...
Word 5. .... = ...

Frequent adverbs Oxford 3000 words

All the words in this lesson are adverbs from the **Oxford 3000** list of important words selected by experts in English teaching. These 3,000 words are shown in the main section of the dictionary in a different color from the other words and with a key symbol 🔑 immediately following.

> **prompt·ly** 🔑 /'prɑmptli/ *adv.* **1** immediately; without delay: *I invited her to dinner and she promptly accepted.* **2** at the time that you have arranged: *We arrived promptly at 12 o'clock.*

> **mean·while** 🔑 /'minwaɪl/ *adv.* during the same time or during the time between two things happening: *Peter was at home studying. Tony, meanwhile, was out with his friends.*

A. Read each sentence and the seven adverbs that follow. Then circle the three adverbs that could complete each sentence.

1. A small fee will be _____ deducted from Zachary's account.
   automatically   greatly   occasionally   regularly   significantly   thickly   widely

2. Madison was _____ employed as a server during 11th and 12th grades.
   actually   alphabetically   continuously   faithfully   mentally   previously   tightly

3. We _____ asked our history teacher for shorter tests.
   formally   politically   potentially   recently   repeatedly   steeply   terribly

4. Prices of textbooks have increased _____.
   coldly   considerably   secretly   slightly   softly   substantially   willingly

5. Another company has offered me a job, but my salary there would be _____ the same as what I'm earning now.
   adequately   angrily   exactly   firmly   locally   roughly   virtually

6. Most of the students were _____ well prepared for their final exam.
   especially   finely   impatiently   gently   obviously   socially   unusually

7. When it was Samantha's turn to answer, she responded _____.
   basically   cheerfully   highly   honestly   immediately   loosely   traditionally

8. Jacob walked _____ into the room, took a seat, and answered the police officer's questions.
   calmly   closely   confidently   entirely   heavily   largely   nervously

9. Yesterday's class began _____ at 8:15.
   particularly   primarily   promptly   relatively   smoothly   temporarily   unexpectedly

10. Emily looked at me _____ and asked me to leave her alone.
    coldly   directly   equally   generously   greatly   sadly   typically

B. Complete the following sentences with the correct adverb from the Word Bank.

WORD BANK

| afterward   ago   even   however   quite   therefore |

1. She arrived here from China only two weeks _____. _____, her English is limited.

2. Around noon, it began to rain _____ heavily. _____, we had to call off the game.

3. Josh and I studied for our math exam. _____, we went to the student union.

4. My teacher said my essay was _____ good. _____, she said it would be _____ better if I made a few changes to my conclusion.

C. New words

Write down any new words that you have learned in this lesson and then look up their definitions.

Word 1. _____ = _____
Word 2. _____ = _____
Word 3. _____ = _____
Word 4. _____ = _____
Word 5. _____ = _____

Frequent prepositions Oxford 3000 words

All the prepositions and words in bold print in this lesson are from the **Oxford 3000** list of important words selected by experts in English teaching. These 3,000 words are shown in the main section of the dictionary in a different color from the other words and with a key symbol 🔑 immediately following.

be·tween[1] 🔑 /brˈtwin/ *prep., adv.* **1** in the space that separates two things, people, etc.: *I was sitting between Anne and Derek.* ♦ *a town between Los Angeles and San Diego* **2** from one place to another and back again: *There aren't any direct flights between here and Calgary.*

through[1] 🔑 /θru/ *prep.* **1** from one end or side of something to the other: *We drove through the center of town.* ♦ *She could see the outline of a tree through the mist.* ♦ *to look through a telescope* ♦ *James cut through the rope.* ♦ *to push through a crowd of people*

A. Correct the **five** sentences that have an incorrect ADJECTIVE + PREPOSITION combination. (If you need more help, look up the entry for the word in **bold** in each sentence.)

1. Many people feel **anxious** on giving a speech. ....
2. She was very **attached** with her grandmother. ....
3. Do you really think she's **capable** of doing something like that? ....
4. Kerri is **afraid** of flying. ....
5. We're not **familiar** to that author's works. ....
6. He is **guilty** for cheating on the exam. ....
7. Most citizens are **opposed** with that plan. ....
8. Who is **responsible** for washing the windows? ....

B. Complete these sentences with the correct preposition for each NOUN + PREPOSITION combination. (If you need more help, look up the entry for the word in **bold** in each sentence.) You will need to use one of the prepositions in **two** different sentences.

WORD BANK | **between   for   in   of   on   to**

1. He has a great **interest** .... African music.
2. Our school has a strict **policy** .... cell phones.
3. The lack of snow had a severe **impact** .... tourism.
4. We did a project as an **alternative** .... a final exam.
5. This incident set off a **chain** .... events that finally led to war.
6. There is a huge **demand** .... more doctors and nurses.
7. Is there much **difference** .... Mexican and European Spanish?

C. Draw lines to form sentences with the correct VERB + PREPOSITION combination. (If you need more help, look up the entry for the word in **bold** in each sentence.)

1. The key **belongs**   about me.
2. Don't **worry**   on me.
3. She is **staring**   at me.
4. They are **relying**   with me.
5. He usually **disagrees**   to me.

Sublists 1 and 2 Academic Word List

The Academic Word List consists of 570 word families that are common in academic writing. In your dictionary these important words are clearly marked with the symbol **AWL** just after the word.

The Academic Word List is organized by frequency into ten sublists. Sublist 1 contains the most common words in the AWL, sublist 2 contains the next most common words, and so on. There are 60 families in each sublist, except for sublist 10 which has 30.

This lesson focuses on word families from sublists 1 and 2.

Example from Sublist 1

> **da·ta** 🔑 **AWL** /ˈdeɪtə; ˈdætə/ *noun* [U, pl.] facts or information: *to collect data* ◆ *The data is/are still being analyzed.*

Example from Sublist 2 (from the word family <u>equate</u>)

> **e·qua·tion** **AWL** /ɪˈkweɪʒn/ *noun* [C] **(MATH)** a statement that two quantities are equal: *Solve the equation 2x + 5 = 11.*

A. Use all three AWL answer choices from sublists 1 and 2 to complete each sentence. The blue words in the sentences are also from these sublists. Use your dictionary to check any meanings of AWL words that you are not sure of.

		AWL answer choices
1.	A **significant** ___source___ of Mr. Ming's **income** is from _____ in local _____ projects.	construction, investments, ~~source~~
2.	When the buyer _____ enough **credit**, the _____ of your new _____ can **occur**.	purchase, residence, obtains
3.	For the **period** from June 15 to October 15, 2010, a rough _____ of companies with _____ **labor** problems is as high as twenty _____.	percent, estimate, major
4.	In our _____, the _____ **authority** that **establishes** most _____ on local issues is a **commission**.	community, policies, primary
5.	This **survey** _____ on the _____ **financial** _____ of studying for a master's degree.	benefits, focuses, potential
6.	The _____ of current **environmental** _____ on the **economy** will _____ from country to country.	impact, research, vary
7.	One **positive** news _____ is that the accident _____ only two **individuals** and that no one was _____.	injured, involved, item
8.	The **process** of _____ the usefulness of an academic **article** is very _____ and _____ a great deal of time and effort.	complex, evaluating, requires
9.	One _____ **method** for working out the **definition** of an unknown word is to _____ the word in _____.	analyze, appropriate, context
10.	Most _____ **select** a new **computer** on the basis of its _____ **features** and the number of _____ it performs.	functions, consumers, design

B. Answer these questions that use AWL vocabulary.

1. What is **normal** body temperature? _____
2. Give two examples of possible **evidence** in a murder case.

   _____
3. What is the **formula** for converting miles to kilometers? _____
4. Name a **tradition** in your family or at your school or work.

   _____
5. What was the **site** of the last Summer Olympics? _____
6. What is the **area** of a square with a side that is 8 inches long? _____
7. What is one possible **consequence** of staying up very late? _____
8. Do you have a favorite **section** of the newspaper? _____

Sublists 3 and 4 Academic Word List

The Academic Word List of 570 word families is organized by frequency into ten sublists, and this lesson focuses on word families from sublists 3 and 4.

Example from Sublist 3
(from the family word <u>immigrate</u>)

im·mi·gra·tion AWL /ˌɪməˈɡreɪʃn/ *noun* [U]
1 entering a country in order to live there: *There are more controls on immigration than there used to be.* ◆ *the Immigration and Naturalization Service*

Example from Sublist 4

code¹ AWL /koʊd/ *noun* **1** [C, U] a system of words, letters, numbers, etc. used instead of other words, letters, etc. so that messages, information, etc. can be kept secret: *They succeeded in breaking/ cracking/deciphering the enemy code* (= in finding out what it was). ◆ *They wrote letters to each other in code.*

A. Use all three AWL answer choices from sublists 3 and 4 to complete each sentence. The blue words in the sentences are also from these sublists. Use your dictionary to check any meanings of AWL words that you are not sure of.

		AWL answer choices
1.	The _____ **goal** of this **document** is to _____ each person's individual _____ in the project.	specify, task, principal
2.	At the _____ **conference** last week, a small _____ of _____ ten percent of the participants voted against the **scheme**.	annual, minority, approximately
3.	In **contrast** to the figures for 1900, recent _____ on _____ reflect the _____ from agriculture to **technology**.	occupations, shift, statistics
4.	**Despite considerable** _____ about the _____ for choosing this year's winner, the committee will need to _____ again in a month to discuss it further.	convene, criteria, debate
5.	An **internal** _____ of the company's accounts _____ several key administrators to the _____ of a large amount of company **funds**.	investigation, links, removal
6.	It is possible to **predict** the **overall** _____ of workers from their _____ toward their _____.	attitude, output, job
7.	Three **obvious** ways of improving your English are to have total _____ to your studies, to _____ on improving your **communication** skills, and to use materials that _____ vocabulary.	concentrate, commitment, stress
8.	If there is _____ **funding**, we will _____ a special **project** on **publishers'** _____ to e-books and other digital products.	reactions, sufficient, undertake
9.	The military _____ that came to power last month has **predictably imposed** a _____ of new laws that _____ special powers to the army.	grant, regime, series
10.	The **corporation** sells a wide range of products but its _____ business still _____ on **domestic** sales; this is _____ why it rarely advertises abroad.	core, apparently, relies

B. Answer these questions that use AWL vocabulary.

1. What are your three favorite **ethnic** food dishes? _____

2. What information can you find on the **label** on a soup can? _____

3. If you opened a new restaurant near here, name two methods you might use to **promote** it. _____

4. What are some typical **comments** you receive from teachers about your written English? _____

5. What methods do your teachers use to **resolve** behavior issues in class?
_____

6. Name one or two companies that **dominate** the clothing market today.
_____

7. What are your **initials**? Does anyone else in your group have the same initials?
_____

8. What kind of book has the greatest number of useful **illustrations** for you as a reader? _____

Sublists 5 and 6 Academic Word List

The Academic Word List of 570 word families is organized by frequency into ten sublists, and this lesson focuses on word families from sublists 5 and 6.

Example from Sublist 5

psy·chol·o·gy **AWL** /saɪˈkɑlədʒi/ *noun* **1** (also *informal* **psych**) [U] the study of the mind and the way that people behave: *child psychology* ⊃ Look at **psychiatry**. **2** [sing.] the type of mind that a person or group of people has

Example from Sublist 6
(from the word family <u>intelligent</u>)

in·tel·li·gence 🔊 **AWL** /ɪnˈtɛlədʒəns/ *noun* [U] **1** the ability to understand, learn, and think: *Examinations are not necessarily the best way to measure intelligence.* ◆ *a person of normal intelligence* ◆ *an intelligence test*

A. Use all three AWL answer choices from sublists 5 and 6 to complete each sentence. The blue words in the sentences are also from these sublists. Use your dictionary to check any meanings of AWL words that you are not sure of.

		AWL answer choices
1.	In our current **psychology** professor's _____, she has _____ **fundamental** ideas we learned about in _____ classes.	challenged, lectures, preceding
2.	If I follow the **instructions** for these eye vitamins _____, the **medicine** will _____ my eyesight so I can see _____ more clearly.	enhance, images, precisely
3.	Our **assignment** is to select two **authors** without _____ the instructor and read a _____ of ten chapters by each of them, _____ to two books.	consulting, equivalent, minimum
4.	Two **prime** _____ of people who _____ a career **overseas** are travel and the _____ of learning a new language.	challenge, motives, pursue
5.	I had to **draft** a new application for a **license** because the committee _____ the previous one , _____ _____ information in my paperwork.	citing, inaccurate, rejected
6.	The chief financial officer _____ that the company **exceeded** legal limits on **external** loans and agreed that it must _____ its _____ better in the future.	acknowledged, monitor, revenue
7.	If you _____ the form in any way, including **substituting** information, you must _____ a _____ written explanation of all your **alterations**.	attach, brief, modify
8.	We all welcome the _____ from **explicit** _____ on the grounds of race and _____ to the greater **diversity** that exists today.	gender, transition, discrimination
9.	The _____ of late payment has **declined** because companies charge a late **fee** as an _____ to pay promptly; _____, many people still pay late	incentive, incidence, nevertheless
10.	In **cooperating** with the authorities, the thief _____ an extensive **network** of criminals who _____ deadly weapons to _____ their victims.	revealed, target, utilize

B. Answer these questions that use AWL vocabulary.

1. How many **generations** of your family are still alive today?
   ....

2. Where do you usually find the **abstract** of an article – at the beginning, in the middle, or at the end? ....

3. What is the chemical **symbol** for oxygen? ....

4. If there is no **trace** of a person, how easy is it to find them?
   ....

5. What do you recommend as the fastest way to **recover** from a cold?
   ....

6. If James wrote some notes in the **margin** of his book, on what part of the page did he write them? ....

7. Which one of the following is a **compound** noun – *homework*, *schedule*, or *discrimination*? ....

8. What is the **ratio** of females to males in your class? ....

Sublists 7 and 8 Academic Word List

The Academic Word List of 570 word families is organized by frequency into ten sublists, and this lesson focuses on word families from sublists 7 and 8.

Example from Sublist 7

mode **AWL** /moʊd/ *noun* [C] **1** (*formal*) a type of something or way of doing something: *a mode of transportation* **2** (used about machines, etc.) a way of operating: *I put the generator in standby mode, so it will be ready in case we need it.*

Example from Sublist 8

de·note **AWL** /dɪˈnoʊt/ *verb* [T] (*formal*) to indicate or be a sign of something; to mean something: *What does [T] denote in this dictionary?*

A. Use all three AWL answer choices from sublists 7 and 8 to complete each sentence. The blue words in the sentences are also from these sublists. Use your dictionary to check any meanings of AWL words that you are not sure of.

		AWL answer choices
1.	The teacher said that the .... of the first **paragraph** in my paper was .... vague and **arbitrary** and that it lacked	clarity, somewhat, topic
2.	Ed Reagan's latest book includes a .... review of recent **global** treaties that might **eventually** .... tax rates after ten .... years of increases.	comprehensive, reverse, successive
3.	A **couple** of .... ago, residents of our state voted to **abandon** the .... of old .... that has mercury in it.	decades, disposal, equipment
4.	I don't watch that TV **channel** .... because of its political ....; when I watch TV, my .... is **definitely** relaxation and not politics.	ideology, priority, solely
5.	In my **classical** literature class, the teacher told me to .... **quotation** marks around all direct quotes in my paper and she can then .... in the school newspaper.	guarantee, insert, publication
6.	This new technique does not .... all hearing problems, but it is an important .... that will **aid** children and **adults** who .... signs of hearing loss.	eliminate, exhibit, innovation
7.	We cannot .... that the evidence **highlighted** by our **chemical** experiment is not ....; in fact, our results are .... to those of a similar test in Germany last year.	deny, identical, unique
8.	.... to what I first .... from talking to my teacher, he **ultimately** liked the paper so much when I **submitted** it that my final .... was A+.	contrary, grade, inferred
9.	Doctors have .... that tomorrow they will .... a report **via** local and national **media** that they have .... a virus that causes heart disease.	confirmed, isolated, release
10.	Sometimes used as **currency** in the past, gold is a valuable .... because there is only a .... amount available, **plus** it is difficult to .... from the earth.	commodity, extract, finite

B. Answer these questions that use AWL vocabulary.

1. Does your dictionary have an **appendix**? If so, where is it? ....

2. Name three ingredients that are **crucial** to writing a good paragraph or essay.
....

3. Which of the following are not part of a country's **infrastructure** – transportation, the water supply, sports facilities? ....

4. How many people in your class have a license to operate a motor **vehicle**? ....

5. If a country has **widespread** poverty, what can you say about people's incomes? ....

6. When I asked my boss if he was planning to leave the company, his answer was **ambiguous**. Did he say yes or no? ....

7. The history teacher discussed the six wars in **random** order. Were the wars discussed in alphabetical or chronological order? ....

8. When you have to write a paragraph or essay, what **guidelines** does your teacher give you?

The Academic Word List of 570 word families is organized by frequency into ten sublists, and this lesson focuses on word families from sublists 9 and 10.

Example from Sublist 9

in·her·ent AWL /ɪnˈhɛrənt; -ˈhɪr-/ adj. inherent (in sb/sth) that is a basic or permanent part of someone or something and that cannot be removed: *The risk of collapse is inherent in any business.*

Example from Sublist 10

in·trin·sic AWL /ɪnˈtrɪnzɪk; -sɪk/ adj. (only *before* a noun) (*formal*) (used about the value or quality of something) belonging to something as part of its nature; basic: *The object has no intrinsic value* (= the material it is made of is not worth anything).

A. Use all three AWL answer choices from sublists 9 and 10 to complete each sentence. The blue words in the sentences are also from these sublists. Use your dictionary to check any meanings of AWL words that you are not sure of.

		AWL answer choices
1.	My trip home should have been **straightforward**, but as I _____ my preparations, I felt an _____ sense of **depression** that I had not _____.	anticipated, commenced, odd
2.	Jackie and I have many _____ friends and **colleagues** who served in the **military**, and we are _____ that it made them more _____ people.	convinced, mature, mutual
3.	After the **revolution**, the _____ "government" was very weak and _____ numerous problems; _____, it did not **collapse**.	encountered, nonetheless, so-called
4.	For the **duration** of his jail sentence, the prisoner was _____ to an **enormous** cell _____ to the guards' office where he _____ no danger to others.	adjacent, confined, posed
5.	According to the **preliminary** data, the behavior of this _____ of doctors was not _____, but the investigation is _____ and more results will be **forthcoming**.	ethical, ongoing, panel
6.	My **inclination** was to remain _____ and do absolutely nothing in order to see whether the **team** _____ at least a _____ of their objectives.	attained, passive, portion
7.	Her love for her husband gradually _____ and she was _____ to be seen with him; **conversely**, he had a **persistent** need to see her until at last he realized that their goals were _____.	diminished, incompatible, reluctant
8.	On _____ of our class, I would like to thank our _____ teacher, Mrs. Montluzin, for her **vision**, her **integrity**, and her _____ into our needs.	behalf, devoted, insight
9.	According to a **manual** _____ from owners' personal accounts, a **medium**-sized car of this type has _____ maintenance costs, _____ some mechanical problems.	compiled, minimal, notwithstanding
10.	The principal caused **controversy** by saying that the school was far too **relaxed** and must _____ certain changes _____ students would have more _____ rules and regulations.	rigid, undergo, whereby

B. Answer these questions that use AWL vocabulary.

1. Michael called to request **accommodations** for a week. What kind of business did he call? _____

2. Which of these is usually the object of the verb **levy** – a business, a storm, or a tax? _____

3. Ashley bought a bookcase with a label that said, "SOME **ASSEMBLY** REQUIRED." What did she have to do? _____

4. The president said, "This plan was **conceived** at a meeting of twenty senators." What did the senators do? _____

5. What is your favorite **format** for a test in this class? _____

6. The Juffs family and the Ackel family booked vacations in Germany, and they just found out that their trips **overlap** by five days. What does this mean? _____

7. Name three electrical **devices** that most people have in their houses. _____

8. If the **bulk** of applications for a particular job were not good, how many do you think were acceptable – 30%, 50%, or 70%? _____

Answer Key

Lesson 1

A. 1. arrow   2. bury   3. deaf   4. embarrass   5. fuel
   6. joy   7. neat   8. onion   9. reward   10. wrapping
   11. youth   12. zero

B. **1.** 1. fact   2. factor   3. factory   4. fasten   5. faucet
   6. feather   7. flat   8. floor   9. flour   10. flow
   11. fork   12. form
   2. 1. o'clock   2. Oct.   3. OK   4. old   5. old-fashioned
   6. once   7. onion   8. online   9. organize
   10. organized   11. ought to   12. owe

C. 1. guard/gypsy   2. petroleum jelly/photography
   3. accreditation/act   4. rate/reactive   5. seed/
   self-inflicted   6. remain/rent   7. dogged/double
   8. untrustworthy/upside down

Lesson 2

A. 1. c   2. e   3. g   4. i   5. f   6. l   7. k   8. d   9. m   10. n

B. 1. <u>ve</u>getable, c.   2. sugary, b.   3. dorm, f.   4. It should
   be "Listen to what she says.", d.   5. unkind, e.   6. No, it
   should be pota**toes**, g.   7. to•mor•row, a.

Lesson 3

A. 1. -, -   2. an, a   3. -, a   4. a, -   5. a, a   6. a, a

B. 1. ---   2. ---   3. on   4. ---   5. to

C. 1. an avid player (*avid* is only used before a noun)
   2. three or more homework assignments (*homework*
   is an uncountable noun)   3. devoid of   4. tells me (for
   orders we use *tell* + infinitive; *say* is not followed by
   the person (or pronoun) that the speaker is talking to)
   5. hounded the suspect (*hound* is a transitive verb)
   6. a sure-fire plan (*sure-fire* is only used before a
   noun)   7. a paralegal (*paralegal* is a countable noun)
   8. these jeans suit me (*suit* is not used in the *–ing* form)
   9. living creature (*alive* is not used before a noun)
   10. These bacteria cause... (*bacteria* is a plural noun)

Lesson 4

A. **1.** 1. explode   2. bribe   3. call sth off
   4. frank   5. stroke   6. main   7. sleepy
   8. stress   9. remarkable   10. fix
   2. 1. uncivilized   2. cloudless   3. inhale
   4. initial   5. inhospitable   6. imprecise
   7. insane   8. dissatisfaction

B. 1. a property   2. inexpensive   3. pick   4. no   5. filthy
   6. bug   7. moist   8. term

Lesson 5

A. a. 1   b. 5   c. 2   d. 3   e. 1   f. 5   g. 4   h. 1   i. 3

B. 1. fan (1)   2. messy (1)   3. messy (3)   4. lighten (1)
   5. mint (3)   6. pound (2)   7. pound (1)   8. messy (2)
   9. lighten (2)   10. mint (1)   11. mint (2)   12. fan (2)

Lesson 6

A. 1. a. crust   b. loaf   2. a. hairbrush, toothbrush, nail
   brush   b. dustpan   3. a. sofa/couch, bench   b. stool
   4. a. peel   b. red and green   5. a. pie chart   b. vertical
   axis and horizontal axis   6. a. hard hat   b. any 3 of
   sombrero, sun hat, cowboy hat, top hat   7. a. ladle
   b. spatula   8. a. you insert a plug into an outlet   b.
   water   9. a. rake   b. saw   10. a. run   b. the discus and
   the javelin

Lesson 7

A. 1. yes   2. no   3. yes   4. yes   5. no   6. yes   7. no
   8. no   9. yes   10. no   11. yes   12. yes   13. no   14. yes
   15. no   16. yes   17. no   18. no   19. yes   20. no

B. 1. in the shade   2. lemons   3. books or the Internet
   4. It's carefully done and very complete.   5. no
   6. north to south   7. blue bonnet   8. shop   9. no
   10. no

Lesson 8

A. 1. no   2. yes   3. no   4. yes   5. yes   6. no   7. yes
   8. yes   9. yes   10. yes   11. no   12. no   13. no   14. no
   15. no   16. no   17. no   18. yes   19. no   20. yes

B. 1. easier   2. information   3. negative   4. Abigail
   5. cars, textiles, kitchen appliances, etc.   6. bad
   7. a pile of books   8. a shallow river; a deep river
   9. above   10. 2 pages long   11. an employer   12. solve

Lesson 9

A. 1. no   2. no   3. no   4. yes   5. no   6. yes   7. yes   8. no
   9. yes   10 no   11. no   12. no   13. no   14. no   15. no
   16. yes   17. no   18. no   19. yes   20. no

B. 1. no   2. a helmet   3. Yugoslavia   4. no   5. no,
   because farms are in the country.   6. tape   7. The first
   meaning of the verb to draw is to make a picture, and
   a drawing is a picture. The second meaning is to pull,
   and a drawer is something you pull out to put things in.
   8. read it immediately   9. a hole or an empty space
   10. a small farm in the countryside   11. a bad thing
   12. a lawyer

Lesson 10

A. 1. no   2. yes   3. no   4. no   5. no   6. yes   7. no   8. yes
   9. no   10 yes   11. no   12. no   13. yes   14. no   15. no
   16. no   17. no   18. yes   19. yes   20. no

B. 1. $1,400   2. negatively   3. a.) to refuse to work b.) to
   attack   4. a washing machine   5. 5 people   6. *Algebra*
   comes from Arabic; *denim* comes from the French for
   a type of material from the town of Nîmes; *quarantine*
   comes from an Italian word for "forty days"; and *salary*
   comes from a Latin word which meant "a Roman
   soldier's allowance to buy salt".   7. a boat or ship
   8. roses, lilies, daises, poppies, tulips, etc.   9. politics
   10. yes   11. no   12. If they put them in their mouths,
   they may choke.

Lesson 11

A. 1. yes 2. no 3. no 4. no 5. yes 6. no 7. yes 8. no 9. no 10 no 11. no 12. no 13. no 14. yes 15. no 16. no 17. no 18. no 19. no 20. no

B. 1 a ditch 2. two or three 3. never 4. yes 5. Wednesday, Thursday, and Friday 6. ban them? allow students to use them all the time? 7. none 8. flu 9. honey, because it's sweet 10. six 11. in a book 12. never

Lesson 12

A. dou**b**t, forei**g**n, su**b**tle, listen, ca**l**m, cas**t**le, mus**c**le, **k**nife

B. 1. occurred 2. perseverance 5. pastime 6. millennium 7. responsible 8. privilege 10. definitely 11. campaign 13. misspell 15. grammar 16. separate 17. believe 18. column (3., 4., 9., 12., and 14. are correct.)

C. 1. accommodate 2. occurred 3. pastime 4. column 5. definitely 6. grammar 7. misspell 8. separate 9. perseverance 10. privilege

Lesson 13

A. lampshade (*noun*), long-term (*adj.*), lifeguard (*noun*), locker room (*noun*), left-handed (*adj.*), low tide (*noun*), leap year (*noun*), laid-back (*adj.*)

B. 1. yes 2. no 3. no 4. maybe! 5. dirt cheap 6. no 7. five cents 8. a thing 9. February 10. Cinderella, Pinocchio, the Wizard of Oz.... 11. eggs 12. none

Lesson 14

A. 1. warm-hearted; true 2. next of kin; true 3. record-breaking; false 4. block letters; false 5. brother-in-law; false 6. sought-after; true 7. ball game; false 8. runner-up; false 9. earth-shattering; false 10. know-how; true 11. cross-examined; true 12. pop quiz; false

B. **1.** 1. a boarding pass 2. to download 3. voice mail 4. a layover 5. a round-trip ticket 6. plastic surgery 7. a checkup 8. user-friendly 9. an X-ray **2.** travel – boarding pass, layover, round-trip ticket; health – plastic surgery, checkup, X-ray; computing – download, voice mail, user-friendly

Lesson 15

Across 1. senior 6. public 8. UFO 9. CV 10. anno 12. Aug. 13. RN 14. TB 15. TM 16. ID 17. Mr. 20. east 21. weight 24. U.S.A. 26. ounce 27. west **Down** 2. information 3. cu 4. Blvd. 5. October 6. pound 7. BC 8. UN 11. N.E. 17. BA 18. Sgt. 19. Mt. 20 ext. 21. Wide 22. TA 23. S.W. 24. U.S. 25. St.

Lesson 16

A. 1. /grin/ 2. /koʊt/ 3. /dʒun/ 4. /ænt, ɑnt/ 5. /ˈdʌzn/

B. 1. c. chair; care, share 2. b. pat; bat, vat 3. b. cup; cub, cuff 4. b. gel; shell, hell 5. a. light; right, ride 6. b. leap; leaf, lip 7. c. tie; shy, thigh 8. a. thick; sick, seek 9. b. ship; sip, sheep 10. c. height; hot, hat

Lesson 17

A. **1. palace** noun, first; **planet** noun, first; **pleasant** adjective, first; **possess** verb; second; **pronounce** verb, second; **painter** noun, first; **painful** adjective, first; **passport** noun, first; **prefer** verb, second; **partner** noun, first; **perform** verb, second; **publish** verb, first

2. Based on this sample, most two-syllable *nouns* and *adjectives* stress the first syllable, and many two-syllable *verbs* stress the second syllable.

B. 1. occur 2. meeting 3. today 4. mention 5. retired 6. forecast 7. unique 8. survive

C. 1. retired 2. unique 3. survive 4. occur 5. meeting 6. forecast 7. mention 8. today

Lesson 18

A. 1. con<u>duct</u> <u>con</u>duct 2. <u>con</u>test con<u>test</u> 3. im<u>port</u> <u>im</u>port 4. <u>in</u>sult in<u>sult</u> 5. ob<u>ject</u> <u>ob</u>ject 6. <u>per</u>mit per<u>mit</u> 7. pro<u>duce</u> <u>pro</u>duce 8. <u>re</u>bel re<u>bel</u> 9. re<u>cord</u> <u>re</u>cord

B. 1. author (1), received (2), rather (1), amount (2), money (1), birthday (1), present (1), partner (1) 2. suspect's (1), reply (2), police (2), questions (1), amazed (2), object (1) 3. instance (1), agree (2), hatred (1), healthy (1), feeling (1), people (1), ignore (2) 4. extreme (2), weather (1), April (1), result (2), damage (1), garden (1), forest (1) 5. Parents (1), teachers (1), sometimes (1), demand (2), children (1), study (1), subjects (1), enjoy (2),

C. Brazil (2), Japan (2), Sweden (1), Turkey (1), China (1), Kenya (1), Peru (2), Jordan (1), Egypt (1), Thailand (1), Kuwait (2), Iceland (1), Chile (1), Iraq (2), Iran (2), Norway (1)

Lesson 19

A. 1. could 2. youth 3. although 4. doubt 5. ought 6. aloud 7. proud 8. routine 9. through 10. though 11. soup 12. should

B. **cloud** 1. encounter 2. proud 3. shout 4. amount **soup** 1. routine 2. wounded 3. through 4. youth **cough** 1. thought 2. ought **young** 1. tough 2. cousin 3. rough **though** 1. although 2. shoulder 3. soul **should** 1. could 2. would

Lesson 20

A. 1. location 2. adhesive 3. restoration 4. greeting
5. denial 6. approach 7. adoption 8. detention
9. cruelty 10. implication 11. extravagance
12. complaint 13. classic 14. security 15. brevity
16. ventilation *or* ventilator

B. 1. gesture 2. replacement 3. repellent 4. depth
5. addition 6. decision 7. forecast 8. display
9. gossip 10. interest 11. rehearsal 12. hindrance

Lesson 21

A. issue - 6. and 11.; lap - 3. and 8.; log - 2. and 4.;
minority - 10. and 12.; quarter - 1. and 9.; race - 5. and 7.

B. 1. course (3) 2. bridge (1) 3. course (1) 4. pack
(2) 5. press (3) 6. story (4) 7. chain (3) 8. pack (3)
9. chain (1) 10. press (1) 11. story (1) 12. bridge (3)

Lesson 22

A. 1. interrupt 2. broadcast 3. offend 4. warn 5. cut
6. stress 7. stabilize 8. emphasize 9. prove
10. picnic 11. rely 12. diversify 13. burglarize
14. conceive 15. map 16. massage

B. 1. got 2. fell 3. quit 4. woke 5. fled 6. set 7. beat
8. sank 9. threw 10. let 11. spun 12. lead 13.
forgave 14. grew 15. dug 16. burst 17. spread 18.
wound up

C. 1. flavor 2. score 3. abbreviate 4. slander 5. confer
6. refund 7. deny

Lesson 23

A. settle - 5. and 10.; issue - 6. and 7.; practice - 3. and 9.;
ground - 2. and 12.; launch - 1. and 4.; back - 8. and
11.

B. 1. missed (3) 2. land (1) 3. bolt (2) 4. holding (1)
5. beamed (3) 6. pick (1) 7. pick (2) 8. bolted (3)
9. missed (2) 10. hold (10) 11. land (3)
12. beaming (1)

Lesson 24

A. 1. additional 2. furious 3. successful 4. shocked
or shocking 5. logical 6. entertaining 7. curly
8. emotional 9. escaped 10. helpful 11. wonderful
12. furry 13. rainy 14. flawed 15. powerful
16. interested and interesting

B. 1. annoying. 2. isolated 3. damaging 4. alarming
5. confused 6. embarrassed 7. promising 8. amused
9. humiliating 10. concerned 11. surprising
12. bored

Lesson 25

A. 1. voluntarily 2. seriously 3. inevitably 4. randomly
5. visually 6. arbitrarily 7. automatically 8. bitterly
9. easily 10. dramatically 11. likely 12. immediately
13. predominantly 14. fast 15. radically 16. properly

B. 1. Unfortunately, nervously 2. originally, fluently
3. lightly, gradually 4. deliberately, quietly
5. substantially, practically

C. 1. Hardly 2. late 3. Lately, hard 4. hardly, late
5. hardly, lately

Lesson 26

A. 1. true 2. false 3. true 4. false 5. false 6. false
7. false 8. true 9. true 10. false 11. false
12. false

B. 1. of, into 2. on, in 3. in, for, for 4. with, about, for
5. between, with, over 6. into, of

Lesson 27

B. 1. outnumbered 2. outdo 3. outlived (or outlasted)
4. outweighed 5. outgrew 6. outlast (or outlive)

C. 1. d. 2. f. 3. b. 4. c. 5. a. 6. e.

D. 1. outgoing 2. outlying 3. outright 4. outrageous
5. outdated

Lesson 28

A. antsy = impatient; bushed = tired; cranky = irritable;
jumbo = very large; jumpy = anxious; laid-back =
relaxed

B. 1. b 2. e 3. g 4. a 5. f 6. i 7. d 8. j 9. h 10. c

Lesson 29

A. change hands = to pass from one owner to another;
split hairs = to pay too much attention in an argument
to differences that are very small and not important;
pull sb's leg = to make fun of someone by trying to
make him/her believe something that is not true; rack
your brains = to try hard to think of something or
remember something; cost an arm and a leg = to cost a
large amount of money; lose face = to lose the respect
of other people

B. 1. hand 2. ear 3. head 4. tongue 5. neck 6. wrist 7. skin
8. fingers

C. 1. e 2. a 3. b 4. g 5. f 6. d 7. c

Lesson 30

A. 1. In the first place 2. all at once 3. At long last
4. on the dot 5. in two 6. in her sixties 7. kill two
birds with one stone 8. Once upon a time

B. 1. no 2. Answers may vary, but most people's
answer will be no. 3. the chunk of cheddar (cheese)
4. positive 5. He is not sure that he wants to go
to Miami. 6. no 7. no 8. October 9. speaking
10. two 11. no 12. no

Lesson 31

A. 1. h 2. a 3. j 4. b 5. f 6. i 7. e 8. d 9. g 10. c

B. 1. off 2. up 3. got 4. looked 5. after 6. up 7. gave
8. out 9. off 10. came 11. up 12. got.

Lesson 32

A. 1. go to, work out at   2. gained, put on   3. have, get
4. a manual, a stick shift   5. find, get   6. resign from,
quit   7. to buy, to pay for   8. $3,000 dollars a month,
a pension   9. at the counter, at the register   10. divide
up, split   11. in cash, by card   12. ask for, get
13. change, switch   14. burn, copy   15. check, collect
16. pack, unpack   17. lets up, stops   18. forecasting,
predicting

B. any one or more of the following: 1. make/get/receive
a phone call; send/receive/get a text   2. have/get a
haircut; be dressed as a pirate   3. be into classical/
jazz/pop/hip-hop; download an album   4. catch a
cold/the flu/a virus/a bug; sprain/twist your ankle
5. insects crawl/fly/bite/sting/swarm; an egg/a chick
hatches

Lesson 33

A. 1. e   2. f   3. b   4. d   5. a   6. c

B. 1. astounded   2. yell   3. calmly   4. foul   5. from now
on

C. 1. foul   2. couple   3. shaky   4. struggle   5. cause
6. now   7. mad   8. mind   9. arm   10. amazing
11. peaceful   12. way

Lesson 34

A. 1. on; true   2. to; false   3. of; false   4. in; true
5. of; true   6. with; false   7. to; false   8. against; false
9. as; true   10. with; true   11. into; false   12. for; true

B. 1. in; b   2. to; a   3. of; b   4. from; b   5. on; b   6. to; a
7. from; b   8. of; b   9. with; a   10. for; b

Lesson 35

A. 1. broadly   2. train   3. fact   4. depletes   5. wide
6. sufficient   7. increasing   8. propel   9. hollow
10. daunting   11. persuade   12. gratefully
13. carefully   14. routine

Lesson 36

A. 1. whisper   2. place   3. slight   4. somewhat   5. prove
6. customer   7. nearby   8. over

B. 1. bill   2. world   3. before   4. somewhat   5. same
6. store, cone   7. ask   8. enough   9. take   10. slight
11. game

Lesson 37

A. 1. j   2. e   3. f   4. b   5. g (or f)   6. h   7. c   8. l   9. d
10. a   11. k   12. i

B. 1. 90   2. 49 square inches   3. two   4. 6   5. 11 and 13
6. no   7. 3^3, 27   8. 4   9. 8   10. add

Lesson 38

A. **creatures**: larva, amphibian, mollusk, primate,
butterfly, parasite
instruments: test tube, laser, circuit breaker,
microscope, beaker, thermometer
metals: copper, nickel, mercury, tungsten, lithium,
uranium
body parts: appendix, kidney, lung, pancreas, liver,
Achilles tendon

B. 1. scale   2. school   3. chlorophyll   4. distill   5. incisors
6. Sediment   7. navel   8. Saliva   9. fern   10. flow chart
11. gills   12. pollen   13. life cycle   14. offspring

Lesson 39

A. 1. W   2. W   3. L   4. W   5. L   6. W   7. W   8. L   9. W
10. W   11. L   12. L   13. L   14. L   15. W   16. W
17. W   18. L   19. L   20. W

B. 1. hold primary elections   2. the Star-Spangled
Banner   3. the U.S. government   4. dealing with
foreign countries   5. National Aeronautics and Space
Administration

C. 1. ballot, polling place, precinct   2. treaty, ratify
3. alien, green card   4. first lady, national anthem
5. veto

D. 1. B   2. C   3. C   4. A   5. A   6. C   7. B   8. B   9. B
10. B   11. C   12. C

Lesson 40

A. **football:** 1. end zone   2. quarterback   3. running back
4. scrimmage   5. tackle   6. touchdown
basketball: 1. backboard   2. dribble   3. shoot
4. slam-dunk
running: 1. marathon   2. lap   3. sprint
tennis: 1. backhand   2. love   3. match   4. racket
5. serve   6. volley
golf: 1. club   2. course   3. green   4. tee
baseball: 1. batter   2. catcher   3. doubleheader
4. home run   5. outfield   6. shortstop   7. strike out

B. 1. field   2. court   3. court   4. course   5. field   6. field

C. 1. a bad thing   2. the pitcher   3. extremely close
4. a stick   5. neither   6. in caves under the ground
7. Little League   8. car racing   9. decathlon   10. two

Lesson 41

A. 1. pace, wage   2. fee, grade   3. pocket, sleeve
4. award, colleague   5. bowl, steam

B. **body parts:** ankle, elbow, heel, shoulder, skin, waist,
wrist
things you wear: fashion, fur, glove, jacket, leather,
silk, underwear
person: consumer, nephew, partner, passenger, sailor,
scientist, soldier
geography: border, desert, hill, ocean, region, slope,
valley

Lesson 42

A. 1. blame, shock   2. reform, rescue   3. crush, ruin
4. burst, sting   5. apologize, complain

B. 1. c   2. b   3. a   4. d   5. a   6. b   7. a   8. c   9. d   10. b

Lesson 43

A. 1. annual, parallel, steep   2. light, rich, sweet
3. contemporary, loud, soft

B. 1. cruel   2. awful   3. grave   4. bitter   5. dull
6. lacking   7. awkward   8. immoral

C. 1. professional   2. reasonable   3. regional
4. weekly   5. suitable   6. original   7. western
8. massive   9. cheerful   10. enjoyable   11. physical
12. comfortable   13. lively   14. northern   15. faithful

Lesson 44

A. 1. automatically, occasionally, regularly   2. actually,
continuously, previously   3. formally, recently,
repeatedly 4. considerably, slightly, substantially
5. exactly, roughly, virtually   6. especially, obviously,
unusually   7. cheerfully, honestly, immediately
8. calmly, confidently, nervously   9. promptly, smoothly,
unexpectedly   10. coldly, directly, sadly

B. 1. ago, Therefore   2. quite, Therefore   3. Afterward
4. quite, However, even

Lesson 45

A. 1. anxious about   2. attached to   5. familiar with
6. guilty of   7. opposed to

B. 1. in   2. on   3. on   4. to   5. of   6. for   7. between

C. 1. belongs to me   2. worry about me   3. staring at me
4. relying on me   5. disagrees with me

Lesson 46

A. 1. source, investments, construction   2. obtains,
purchase, residence   3. estimate, major, percent
4. community, primary, policies   5. focuses, potential,
benefits   6. impact, research, vary   7. item,
involved, injured   8. evaluating, complex, requires
9. appropriate, analyze, context   10. consumers,
design, functions

B. 1. anywhere between 97.7°F and 99°F   2. a witness to
the crime, fingerprints on the murder weapon, film from
a video camera, etc.   3. multiply the number of miles
by 8 and divide by 5   4. your own answer   5. Beijing
in 2008, London in 2012   6. 64 square inches
7. oversleeping, being very tired in the morning, etc.
8. the sports section, the financial section, etc.

Lesson 47

A. 1. principal, specify, task   2. annual, minority
approximately   3. statistics, occupations, shift
4. debate, criteria, convene   5. investigation, links,
removal   6. output, attitude, job   7. commitment,
concentrate, stress   8. sufficient, undertake, reactions
9. regime, series, grant   10. core, relies, apparently

B. 1. your own answer   2. the ingredients, instructions
on how to prepare it, etc.   3. advertising on TV and in
the newspapers, giving special offers, etc.   4.–7. your
own answers   8. a cookbook, a textbook, a picture
dictionary, etc.

Lesson 48

A. 1. lectures, challenged, preceding   2. precisely,
enhance, images   3. consulting, minimum, equivalent
4. motives, pursue, challenge   5. rejected, citing,
inaccurate   6. acknowledged, monitor, revenue
7. modify, attach, brief   8. transition, discrimination,
gender   9. incidence, incentive, nevertheless
10. revealed, utilize, target

B. 1. your own answer   2. at the beginning   3. O
4. not very easy   5. stay in bed, take vitamins, etc.
6. the side   7. homework   8. your own answer

Lesson 49

A. 1. topic, somewhat, clarity   2. comprehensive, reverse,
successive   3. decades, disposal, equipment   4. solely,
ideology, priority   5. insert, guarantee, publication
6. eliminate, innovation, exhibit   7. deny, unique,
identical   8. contrary, inferred, grade   9. confirmed,
release, isolated   10. commodity, finite, extract

B. 1. If it does, it's at the end.   2. knowledge of the
subject, focus, clarity of expression, etc.   3. sports
facilities   4. your own answer   5. They are mainly very
low.   6. It wasn't clear.   7. neither   8. your own answer

Lesson 50

A. 1. commenced, odd, anticipated   2. mutual, convinced,
mature   3. so-called, encountered, nonetheless
4. confined, adjacent, posed   5. panel, ethical, ongoing
6. passive, attained, portion   7. diminished, reluctant,
incompatible   8. behalf, devoted, insight   9. compiled,
minimal, notwithstanding   10. undergo, whereby, rigid

B. 1. a hotel   2. a tax   3. fit the parts together   4. form
the plan in their minds   5. your own answer   6. they
will be there at the same time   7. washing machines,
vacuum cleaners, televisions, computers, etc.   8. 30%

Wordlist

This is a list of all the words that are taught in the 50 lessons. The words in **blue** are from the **Oxford 3000**™ list and the words with an asterisk (*), from the Academic Word List.

a, an
abandon*
abbreviate
abbreviation
about
above
abroad
absolutely
abstract*
academic*
accept
acceptable
accident
accidentally
accommodate*
accommodation*
accompany*
according to
account
accurate*
accurately*
achieve*
acknowledge*
across
action
activity
actual
actually
adapt*
add
addition
additional
adequately*
adhere
adhesive
adjacent*
adjective
administrator*
admire
adopt
adoption
adult*
adverb
advertise
advertisement
advice
advise
affect*
afford
afraid
after
afternoon
afterward
again
against
age
ago
agree
agreement
agriculture
aid*
AIDS
air
aircraft
airport
alarm
alarming
album
algebra
alien
alive
all
allergic

allow
almost
alone
along
aloud
alphabetical
alphabetically
already
alteration*
alternative*
although
always
amazed
amazing
ambiguous*
amoeba
amount
amphibian
amused
amusing
analyze*
ancestor
ancient
and
anger
angle
angrily
angry
animal
ankle
annoy
annoyed
annoying
annual*
another
answer
anthem
anticipate*
antsy
anxiety
anxious
any
anymore
anyone
anything
apartment
apologize
apparently*
appeal
appear
appearance
appendix*
apple
appliance
application
apply
appreciate*
approach*
appropriate*
approximate*
approximately*
April
arbitrarily*
arbitrary*
ardent
area*
argue
argument
arm
arms
army
around
arrest

arrive
arrow
arson
art
article
artist
as
ashamed
ask
asleep
assembly*
assignment*
assist*
assistant*
assume*
astound
athlete
atmosphere
attach*
attempt
attendant
attention
attentively
attain*
attitude*
attorney
audience
August
aunt
author*
authority*
automatic*
automatically*
available*
average
avid
avoid
award
aware*
away
awful
awkward
axis
baby
bachelor
back
backboard
backhand
backpack
backward
bacteria
bad
bag
baggage
bake
balance
bald
ball
ball game
ballot
ban
banana
bank
banner
bar
barber
barbershop
bargain
bark
barrier
base
baseball

basically
basis
basket
basketball
bat
baton
batter
battery
battle
bayou
be
beach
beaker
bean
bear
beat
beautiful
because
become
bed
bedroom
bee
beef
before
begin
beginning
behalf*
behave
behavior
behind
being
believe
belly button
belong
below
beltway
bench
beneath
benefit*
beret
best
better
between
beyond
bias*
bicycle
big
bike
bill
bird
birth
birthday
bite
bitter
bitterly
blade
blame
blank
block
block letters
blond
blood
blossom
blow
blue
boarding pass
boat
body
bold
bomb
book
bookcase
boot

border
bored
borrow
boss
both
bother
bottom
bound
bowl
box
boy
boyfriend
brain
brainwash
branch
bread
break
breath
breathe
breed
brevity*
bribe
brick
bridge
brief*
brilliant
brim
broadcast
broadly
broccoli
broken
brother
brother-in-law
brown
brush
bug
building
bulk*
burglar
burglarize
burn
burst
bury
bus
bush
bushed
business
busy
but
butter
butterfly
buy
buyer
by
cabinet
cake
calcium
calculate
call
calm
calmly
camera
campaign
can
canal
cancel
cancer
candid
candidate
candy
capable*
capital
capture

car
card
care
career
careful
carefully
carelessly
caress
carrot
cart
case
cash
cast
castle
catch
catcher
cause
cave
ceiling
cell
cell phone
cent
ceremony
certain
certainly
chain
chair
challenge*
championship
chance
change
channel*
chapter*
character
charge
charity
chart*
cheap
cheat
check
checkup
cheddar
cheek
cheer
cheerful
cheerfully
cheese
chemical*
chewing gum
chicken
chief
child
children
chin
chlorophyll
choice
choose
chronological
chunk
circle
circuit breaker
cite*
citizen
city
civilized
claim
clap
clarity*
class
classic*
classical*
classification
classified ad

classmate
clavicle
clean
clear
clearly
clerk
clever
climate
climb
clip
clone
close
closely
clot
clothes
clothing
cloud
cloudless
cloudy
club
coat
coffee
coin
colander
cold
coldly
collapse*
collarbone
colleague*
collect
college
color
colorful
column
combination
come
comfort
comfortable
commence*
comment*
commission*
commit*
commitment*
committee
commodity*
common
commonly
communication*
community*
company
compare
compensate*
competition
competitor
compile*
complain
complaint
complex*
compound*
comprehensive*
computer*
conceive*
concentrate*
conception*
concern
concerning
conclude*
conclusion*
condition
conduct*
cone
confer*
conference*

confess
confident
confidently
confine*
confirm*
confused
congress
consequence*
consider
considerable*
considerably*
consideration
consistent*
constantly*
construction*
consult*
consumer*
contain
contemporary*
content
contest
context*
continuously
contrary*
contrast*
contribute*
control
controversy*
convene*
conversely*
convince*
convinced*
cook
cooperate*
cope
copper
copy
copycat
core*
cornea
corporation*
correct
cost
cottage
cotton
couch
cough
could
counter
country
countryside
county
couple*
coupon
course
court
cousin
cover
covering
cowboy
coworker
cranky
crawl
crazy
create*
creativity*
creature
credit*
crime
criminal
criterion (criteria)*
cross
cross-examine
crossword
crowded
crucial*
cruel
cruelty
crush
crust
cub

cube
cubic
cuff
cup
cure
curious
curl
curly
currency*
current
curriculum vitae
customer
cut
CV
cycle*
dad
dagger
damage
damp
danger
dangerous
data*
date
daughter
daunting
dawn
day
dead
deadly
deaf
deal
debate*
debt
decade*
decathlon
decay
decide
decimal
decision
decline*
decoration
deduct
deep
deeply
definitely*
definition*
degree
delay
delicate
delight
deliver
delve
demand
denial*
denim
denominator
deny*
depend
deplete
depression*
depth
derivative*
derive*
describe
desert
deserve
design*
desk
desperately
despite*
dessert
detail
detain
detention
device*
devoid
devote*
devoted*
diagram
dictator

dictionary
diet
difference
different
difficult
dig
digital
diminish*
dinner
direct
direction
directly
dirt
dirty
disagree
discover
discrimination*
discus
discuss
discussion
disease
dish
dislike
display*
disposal*
dissatisfaction
distance
distill
ditch
diverse*
diversify*
diversity*
divide
do
doctor
document*
dog
dollar
domestic*
dominate*
donate
door
dorm
dormitory
dot
doubleheader
doubt
down
download
downtown
dozen
draft*
dramatic*
dramatically*
draw
drawer
drawing
drench
dress
dribble
drill
drink
drive
driver
driving
drop
drowsy
due
dull
duration*
during
dustpan
dusty
duty
DVD
each
eagle
ear
early
earn
earth

earth-shattering
ease
easily
east
eastern
easy
eat
e-book
economy*
edge
edition*
editor*
education
effect
efficiently
effort
egg
eighth
elbow
election
electrical
electricity
eliminate*
else
e-mail
embarrass
embarrassed
embarrassment
emerge*
emergency
emotion
emotional
emphasis*
emphasize*
empire
employ
employee
employer
employment
empty
encounter*
encourage
end
enemy
engineering
English
enhance*
enjoy
enjoyable
enjoyment
enormous*
enough
ensure*
enter
entertain
entertaining
entertainment
entire
entirely
entitle
environmental*
equal
equally
equation*
equipment*
equivalent*
escape
especially
essay
establish*
estimate*
ethical*
ethnic*
European
evaluate*
evaluation*
even
evening
event
eventually*
ever

every
everyone
everything
evidence*
evident*
evil
exactly
exam
examine
example
exceed*
exclusively*
excuse
executive
exercise
exhale
exhibit*
exist
exit
expectancy
experience
experiment
expert*
explain
explanation
explicit*
explode
exposure*
expression
extension
extensive
external*
extract*
extraordinary
extravagance
extravagant
extreme
extremely
eye
eyesight
face
facility*
fact
factor*
factory
fail
failure
faith
faithful
faithfully
fall
fame
familiar
family
famous
fan
fancy
fang
far
fare
far-fetched
farm
farmer
fashion
fast
fasten
father
faucet
favor
favorite
feather
feature*
February
fee*
feed
feel
feeling
female
fence
ferment
fern

few
fiber
field
fifty
figure
film
filthy
fin
final*
finally*
financial*
find
finely
finger
fingerprint
finish
finite*
fire
firecracker
firm
firmly
first
fish
five
fix
flame
flash
flat
flavor
flaw
flawed
flee
flesh
flight
flood
floor
flour
flow
flower
flu
fluently
fly
foam
focus*
foliage
follow
food
foot
football
for
force
forecast
foreign
forest
foretell
forgive
fork
form
formal
formally
format*
former
formerly
formula*
forthcoming*
fortune
foster
foul
found*
four
fraction
framework*
frank
frantically
freedom
freeze
freezer
frequently
fresh
freshen
freshly

Friday
friend
friendly
frighten
from
front
frozen
fruit
fry
fuel
full
fume
fun
function*
fund*
fundamental*
funding*
funeral
funnel
fur
furious
furry
further
fury
future
gain
game
gap
garden
gardening
gas
gasoline
gel
gender*
generally
generate*
generation*
generous
generously
gentle
gently
genuine
geography
gesture
get
gift
gill
girl
give
glad
global*
glove
glucose
go
goal*
gold
golf
good
goods
gossip
government
governor
grade*
gradually
grammar
grandfather
grandma
grandmother
grant*
grape
grapefruit
graph
grateful
gratefully
grave
gravity
gray
great
greatly
green
greet

greeting
grin
ground
group
grow
grubby
guarantee*
guard
guess
guest
guideline*
guilty
gulf
gum
gun
guy
gym
habit
haggle
hair
hairbrush
haircut
half
hamburger
hammer
hand
handful
handle
hang
happen
happiness
happy
hard
hardly
harm
harmful
harmless
harsh
hat
hatch
hatred
have
he
head
heal
healthy
hear
heard
hearing
heart
heat
heavily
heel
height
hell
helmet
help
helpful
her
herbivore
here
hey
high
highlight*
highly
high-rise
hill
him
hinder
hindrance
hip-hop
his
historian
history
hit
hold
hole
hollow
holocaust
home
homeowner

homework
honest
honestly
honey
hope
horizontal
horse
hospitable
hospital
hot
hotel
hound
house
how
however
huge
human
humiliating
humor
humorous
hunt
hurriedly
hurt
husband
I
ice
ice cream
idea
ideal
identical*
identification*
identify*
identity*
ideology
idiom
if
ignore*
ill
illegal*
illness
illustrate*
illustration*
image*
immediate
immediately
imminent
immoral
immunize
impact*
impatient
impatiently
implication*
imply*
import
important
impose*
impossible
imprecise*
impress
improve
in
inaccurate*
inappropriate*
incentive*
inch
incidence*
incident*
incisor
inclination*
include
including
income*
incompatible*
increase
incredibly
indicate*
individual*
inevitable*
inevitably*
inexpensive
infer*

inform
informal
information
infrastructure*
ingredient
inhale
inherent*
inhospitable
initial*
injure*
injured*
injury*
innocent
innovation*
insane
insect
insert*
inside
insight*
install
instance*
instead
instruction*
instructor*
instrument
insult
insurance
integer
integrity*
interact*
interest
interested
interesting
intermediate*
internal*
the Internet
interrupt
interruption
into
intransitive
invention
invest*
investigate*
investigation*
investment*
involve*
involved*
involvement*
irregular
irritable
isolated*
isosceles triangle
issue*
isthmus
it
item*
jacket
jail
jam
January
javelin
jazz
jeans
jelly
jewelry
job*
joy
jumbo
jump
jumpy
June
jungle
just
keep
key
kick
kid
kidney
kill
killer
kilometer

kind
kitchen
knife
knight
know
know-how
knowledge
koala
label*
labor*
lack
lacking
ladle
lady
lagoon
laid-back
lake
lamp
lampshade
lane
language
lap
large
largely
larva
laser
last
late
lately
launch
law
lawyer
lay
layer*
layover
lead
leaf
league
leak
lean
leap
leap year
learn
least
leather
leave
lecture*
left
left-handed
leg
legal*
lemon
length
less
lesser
lesson
let
letter
level
levy*
library
license*
lie
life
lifeguard
light
lighten
lightly
like
likely
lily
limit
limited
line
link*
lip
liquid
listen
literature
lithium
little

live
lively
liver
living
load
loaf
loan
local
locally
locate*
location*
locker room
lodge
log
logic*
logical*
lonely
long
long-term
look
loosely
lose
loss
lost
lot
loud
love
low
low tide
loyal
luggage
lukewarm
lunch
lung
machine
mad
magical
mail
main
mainly
maintenance*
major*
majority*
make
make-believe
male
mall
mammal
man
manner
manual*
manufacture
many
map
marathon
March
margin*
mark
marked
market
married
marry
marsh
mash
mass
massage
massive
master
match
material
math
mature*
may
mayonnaise
me
meadow
mean
meaning
means
measure
mechanical

media*
medicine
medieval
medium*
meeting
mentally*
mention
menu
merchandise
mercury
mess
message
messy
metal
meteorologist
method*
microscope
middle
midnight
might
mile
military*
milk
millennium
mind
minimal*
minimum*
minor*
minority*
mint
minute
misspell
moat
mode*
modern
modify*
moist
mollusk
mom
Monday
money
monitor*
monkey
month
morally
more
morning
mosquito
most
motive*
motor
mound
mount
mountain
mouse
mouth
move
movie
Mr.
Mrs.
much
multiple
multiply
murder
muscle
museum
music
must
mustard
mutual*
my
nail brush
naked
name
narrow
NASA
nasty
nation
national
navel
NBA

near
nearby
nearly
neat
neck
need
negative*
negatively*
negotiate
neighbor
neighborhood
nephew
nervous
nervously
network*
nevertheless*
new
news
newspaper
next
next of kin
nice
nickel
night
no
nonetheless*
nonsense
noon
normal*
normally*
north
northeast
northern
not
note
nothing
notwithstanding*
noun
now
nuclear*
number
numerator
numerous
nurse
nut
nuts
o'clock
object
objective*
observe
obtain*
obvious*
obviously*
occasionally
occupation*
occupy*
occur*
occurrence*
ocean
October
odd*
of
off
offend
offense
offer
office
officer
official
offspring
often
oh
oil
OK
old
old-fashioned
Olympic
on
once
one
ongoing*

onion
online
only
onto
open
operate
opinion
opponent
oppose
opposed
opposite
or
order
ordinal
organ
organize
origin
original
originally
other
ought to
ounce
our
out
outage
outburst
outcast
outdo
outdated
outer
outfield
outgoing
outgrow
outlast
outlaw
outlet
outline
outlive
outlook
outlying
outnumber
output*
outrage
outrageous
outright
outrun
outside
outstanding
outstretched
outweigh
oven
over
overall*
overlap*
overseas*
owe
own
owner
oxygen
pace
pack
page
pain
painful
paint
painter
pair
palace
pan
pancreas
panel*
paper
paperwork
paragraph*
paralegal
parallel*
parasite
parent
park
parrot
part

participant*
particular
particularly
partner*
party
pass
passenger
passive*
passport
past
pastime
pat
patience
patient
pattern
pay
payment
peaceful
peak
pedal
peel
peeler
pelvis
penalty
pension
pentathlon
people
percent*
percentage*
perfect
perfectly
perform
peril
period*
periodic*
permanent
permanently
permit
perpendicular
perseverance
persistent*
person
personal
personality
personally
persuade
pet
petal
phase*
phone
photo
phrase
physics
physical*
pick
pickle
picnic
picture
pie
pie chart
piece
pig
pile
pilgrim
pilot
pincer
pink
pipe
pirate
pistachio
pit
pitcher
place
plain
plan
planet
plankton
plant
plastic
plastic surgery
plateau

play
player
pleasant
please
plot
plug
plumbing
plunger
plural
plus*
pocket
point
pointed
poison
pole
police
policy*
political
politically
politics
pollen
polling place
pond
pool
poor
pop
pop quiz
poppy
popular
portion*
portray
pose*
position
positive*
positively*
possess
possible
poster
potato
potential*
potentially*
pound
poverty
powder
power
powerful
practically
practice
prairie
praise
preceding*
precinct
precise*
precisely*
predict*
predictably*
predominant*
predominantly*
prefer
pregnant
preliminary*
preparation
prepare
preposition
present
preserve
president
press
pretty
previous*
previously*
price
primarily*
primary*
primate
prime*
principal*
printing
prior*
priority*
prisoner

privilege
probably
problem
process*
produce
product
profession
professional*
professor
profit
program
prohibit*
prohibition*
project*
promising
promote*
prompt
promptly
pronounce
proof
propel
proper
properly
property
protection
protest
proud
prove
provide
providing
psychology*
public
publication*
publish*
publisher*
pull
punctual
punish
punishment
purchase*
pure
pursue*
push
put
puzzle
qualified
quality
quantity
quarantine
quarrel
quarter
quarterback
quarterfinal
question
quiet
quietly
quit
quite
quotation*
quote*
race
racing
rack
racket
radical*
radically*
radio
railroad
rain
rainy
rake
ram
random*
randomly*
range*
rap
rare
rarely
rat
rate
rather

ratify
ratio*
raw
reach
react*
reaction*
read
reader
readily
real
realize
really
reason
reasonable
rebel
receipt
receive
recent
recently
recommend
record
record-breaking
recover*
red
red-eye
reflect
reform
reformation
refund
refusal
refuse
regime*
region*
regional*
register*
regret
regularly
regulation*
rehearsal
rehearse
reject*
relate
related
relation
relatively
relaxation*
relaxed*
release*
relevant*
reliable*
reliably*
religion
reluctant*
rely*
remain
remarkable
remember
remote
removal*
renovate
rent
repair
repeatedly
repel
repellent
replace
replacement
reply
report
request
require*
rescue
research*
researcher*
reservation
residence*
resident*
resign
resolve*
respect
respond*

responsible
restaurant
restoration*
restore*
result
retire
retired
reveal*
revenue*
reverse*
review
revolution*
revolutionary*
reward
rewrite
rice
rich
ride
right
rightly
rigid*
rigorous
risk
rival
river
room
root
rose
rough
roughly
round
round trip
routine
row
royal
rub
rude
ruin
rule
ruler
run
runner
runner-up
running
rust
sadly
safe
sail
sailor
salary
sale
saliva
salt
same
sandwich
sane
satisfaction
sauce
saw
say
saying
scale
scandal
scared
scene
schedule*
scheme*
school
scientific
scientist
scissors
score
scratch
screw
screwdriver
scrimmage
seat
second
secret
secretary
secretly

section*
secure*
security*
sediment
see
seed
seek*
seem
select*
sell
seller
semester
senator
send
senior
sense
sensible
sensitive
sentence
separate
sergeant
series*
serious
seriously
serve
server
service
set
settle
seven
several
severe
severely
shade
shadow
shaky
shall
shallow
shape
share
shatter
she
sheep
sheet
shelf
shell
shift*
shiny
ship
shirt
shock
shocking
shoe
shoot
shop
shopper
shopping
short
shortstop
shot
should
shoulder
shout
show
shut
shy
sick
side
sign
signature
significant*
significantly*
silence
silk
similar*
since
sincere
sing
singer
sink
sip

sister
sit
site*
sitting
situation
six
sixteen
sixty
size
skill
skin
sky
slam-dunk
slander
slap
sleep
sleepy
sleeve
slice
slight
slightly
slope
small
smash
smile
smoke
smoothly
sneaker
snow
so
soar
so-called*
soccer
socially
society
sock
sofa
soft
softly
software
soil
soldier
solely*
solid
solution
solve
sombrero
some
somebody
someone
something
sometimes
somewhat*
son
soon
sorry
sought-after
soul
sound
soup
sour
source*
south
southern
space
span
spare
spatula
speak
special
specific*
specify*
spectacular
speech
spelunking
spend
spider

spill
spin
spine
split
sport
sprain
spread
spring
sprint
square
St.
stabilize*
stable*
stage
stamp
stand
standard
staple
star
stare
start
starve
state
statement
statistic*
statue
status*
stay
steady
steal
steam
steep
steeply
step
stick
sticky
stiffly
stifle
still
sting
stone
stool
stop
store
storm
story
stove
straight
straightforward*
strait
stream
street
strength
stress*
strict
strike
stroke
strong
structure*
struggle
student
study
stupid
subject
submit*
substance
substantially
substitute*
subtle
subtract
succeed
success
successful
successive*
such
sudden
suddenly

sue
suffer
sufficient*
sufficiently*
sugar
sugary
suit
suitable
suitcase
sum*
summary*
summer
sun hat
sunny-side up
sunset
super
superiority
supplement*
supply
support
supporter
sure
sure-fire
surge
surgery
surname
surprise
surprised
surprising
surround
survey*
survive*
suspect
swallow
swarm
swear
sweat
sweep
sweet
swell
switch
swollen
syllable
symbol*
table
tablet
tackle
take
talent
talk
tape*
target*
task*
taste
tax
TB
tea
teach
teacher
team*
tear
technique*
technology*
tee
teenager
telephone
television
tell
temperature
temporarily*
ten
tendency
tendon
tennis
tension*
tentacle
tenth

term
terribly
test
text*
textbook
textile
than
thank
that
the
their
them
then
theoretical*
theory*
there
therefore
thermometer
these
they
thick
thickly
thief
thigh
thing
think
third
this
thorough
those
though
thought
thousand
threat
threaten
three
threw
through
throughout
throw
thunder
Thursday
ticket
tide
tie
tightly
time
tiny
tip
tire
tired
title
to
today
together
tomato
tomorrow
tone
tongue
tonight
too
took
tool
toothbrush
top
top hat
topic*
torrential
total
touch
touchdown
touching
tough
tourism
tourist
toward
towel

town
toy
trace*
track
trademark
tradition*
traditionally*
traffic
train
transformation*
transition*
transitive
transportation*
travel
treat
treaty
tree
triangle
trip
trouble
truly
try
tube
tuberculosis
Tuesday
tulip
tungsten
turn
TV
twenty
twist
two
type
typical
typically
UFO
ultimately*
UN
uncivilized
uncle
under
undergo*
underline
understand
undertake*
underwear
unexpectedly
unfair
unfairly
unfit
unfortunately
unfriendly
unidentified
union
unique*
unite
united
unkind
unknown
unpack
until
unusual
unusually
up
upcoming
upon
upper
upset
uranium
urban
urgent
us
use
used
used to
useful
usefulness

user
user-friendly
usual
usually
utensil
utilize*
vacation
vacuum
vague
valley
valuable
value
van
variety
vary*
vegetable
vehicle*
ventilate
ventilation
ventilator
verb
vertical
very
veto
via*
vice versa
victim
video
virtually*
virus
visible*
vision*
visit
visitor
visual*
visually*
vitamin
vivid
vocabulary
voice
voice mail
volley
volume*
voluntarily*
voluntary*
vote
wage
waist
wait
waiter
wake
walk
wall
wallop
want
war
warm
warm-hearted
warn
warning
wash
washing machine
watch
water
watermelon
way
we
weak
wealth
weapon
wear
weather
web
website
wedding
Wednesday
week

weekly
weight
weird
welcome
well
went
west
western
wet
what
wheel
when
where
whereby*
whether
which
while
whisk
whisper
who
whole
why
wide
widely
widespread*
width
wife
will
willing
willingly
win
wind
window
winner
winter
wire
wish
with
withdraw
within
without
wolf
wonder
wonderful
wood
word
work
worker
working
world
worried
worry
worth
would
wound
wow
wrap
wrist
write
writing
written
wrong
X-ray
yawn
year
yell
yellow
yes
yesterday
yet
you
young
your
youth
zero
zone
zoo